Intermediate Language Skills

WRITING

Michael Carrier

HODDER AND STOUGHTON
LONDON SYDNEY AUCKLAND TORONTO

Acknowledgements

The publishers would like to thank the following for permission to reproduce or adapt copyright material:

Syndication International Ltd
The Civil Service Commission
The Essex County Standard
The Evening Gazette
Bricent Language Courses Ltd
Brooke Bond Oxo Ltd
Punch
Dateline International Ltd
The National Magazine Company Ltd
Sovereign Holidays
Times Newspapers Limited
British Rail
Adrians Estate Agents
Leatherborne Ltd
The Blue Boar Hotel, Maldon
Eylure Ltd
Ashe Laboratories
Camera Press Ltd
Mr J Feiffer
Mr C G Davis
Mr T Parks ('Larry')
The Controllers, Her Majesty's Stationery Office
Embassy of the United States of America
Thai Airlines International
Courier Printing and Publishing Services Ltd

Carrier, M.
  Intermediate language skills.
  1. English language — Writing
  2. English language — Study and teaching —
  Foreign students
  I. Title
  808'042   PE1128.A2/

ISBN 0 340 24408 9

First published 1981
Copyright © M. Carrier 1981

Reprinted 1984

Printed in Hong Kong for Hodder and Stoughton Educational, a division of Hodder and Stoughton Ltd, Mill Road, Dunton Green, Sevenoaks, Kent, by Colorcraft Ltd.

Contents

Introduction to students   5

Introduction to teachers   6

Unit 1   Informal letters   8
Unit 2   Giving information   12
Unit 3   Describing people   18
Unit 4   Describing places/objects   22
Unit 5   Describing the past   26
Unit 6   Comparing   30
Unit 7   Invitations   34
Unit 8   Preferences and choices   38
Unit 9   Instructions   41
Unit 10   Future plans   45
Unit 11   Formal letters   51
Unit 12   Reporting   55
Unit 13   Summarising   58
Unit 14   Giving advice   63
Unit 15   Persuading   68
Unit 16   Describing processes   72
Unit 17   Narrative/telling a story   78
Unit 18   Expressing opinions   83
Unit 19   Agreeing/disagreeing   86
Unit 20   Building an argument   90

Keys to exercises   93

Introduction to students

Here are some notes to help you understand the course, and what you can learn from it.

The book is designed to help you improve your written English. It gives you practice in reading and understanding, re-organising the language you already know, and writing about a variety of topics in many different ways.

The book is designed for students who have already studied English to Intermediate level, and wish to take a written examination in English, such as the Cambridge First Certificate in English. The material at the beginning of the book is easier than this level, but by the end of the book students should have reached the level of the First Certificate. This course, however, does not teach you everything you need for the examination — it concentrates on your written English.

How the book is organised

There are 20 Units, and each one contains different types of exercise. They are nearly all organised like this:

A Texts, diagrams, pictures etc to give you the information you need to write about a particular subject. The text also gives you examples of the language you will need.

B Vocabulary — explanations of words you may not know.

C Comprehension — questions to check whether you have understood the text.

D Analysis — more difficult, detailed questions about the information in the text.

E Inference — these questions give you practice in finding out more from texts. Often, there is some piece of information which is not stated clearly in a text. But you can work it out from hints or clues which the text gives.

F Discussion — these questions give you practice in thinking and talking about the wider meaning of the text/topic, and suggest what other related topics you could think about.

G Language Practice — the examples given here show you how to change sentences around, and construct more complicated sentences.

H Writing Practice — this series of exercises gives

you practice in written English in different ways, and teaches you the special forms you need to write letters or summaries.

I Writing Task — after you have done the Writing Practice exercises you will be able to do one or more of the Writing Tasks, using the information and the language you have learned earlier in the Unit. Tasks include writing a letter, a report, summarising, describing and comparing things.

How to use the book

You should work through all the Units, in the order they appear in the book. They are graded — this means the Units at the beginning are easier than the ones at the end of the book.

If you are working through the book with a teacher, then he (or she) will tell you which sections of each Unit to spend more time on, and which to leave out if you are short of time. You should still work on your own as well, by using the vocabulary notes to study the texts in advance. Also, some of the exercises have the answers printed at the back of the book, so you can do them on your own, and then check the answers yourself. But ask your teacher first. The exercises with answers are marked with this symbol: *

If you are working on your own, without a teacher, then you must decide yourself which exercises to do. If you have a lot of time, you should do them all, but otherwise spend more time on Sections A, B, C, G, H, I. When you have written the exercises, you can check the ones marked * yourself. For your longer pieces of writing you should try and find a teacher or someone who speaks good English to read through and correct them.

For extra practice, you should read as much English as you can, to increase your understanding and expand your vocabulary. It would be a good idea to find a penfriend in an English-speaking country so you can practise your letter-writing as well.

Good luck with your writing!

Introduction to teachers

Course objectives

This course has been designed for students at intermediate level, who are working towards the Cambridge First Certificate examination, or following a course at a similar level. The Units are graded from an average intermediate level in the first Units to a level equivalent to First Certificate at the end of the book.

The course aims to:

a develop students' competence in the use of specific functions of language such as expressing an opinion, giving instructions

b develop students' understanding of the differences between written and spoken English forms

c develop and practise specific writing skills, such as composing a letter, summarising, writing a report.

The course material also develops and practises these general language skills:

a reading for information and understanding (extensive and intensive reading)

b vocabulary extension in the topic areas dealt with in the Units

c oral summary of text material

d oral presentation of information and argument, for discussion

e oral interpretation of visual material.

Organisation of the course

There are 20 Units in the course, each consisting of the following categories of exercise and practice material. There are slight variations in some Units, but the format is essentially:

A Text and/or visual stimulus — to provide students with the information they need for the Writing Practice, along with examples of the written forms they will need to use.

B Vocabulary notes — simple explanations of lexical items from the text.

C Comprehension questions

D Analysis questions

E Inference questions

F Discussion suggestions

G Language Practice exercises

H Writing Practice exercises

I Writing Task(s)

How to use the course

Each Unit contains a wide range of practice material, and it may not be possible to cover all the work in class in situations where class-time is limited. The teacher should then decide which exercises are most appropriate to the specific needs of his students, and which can be omitted. Similarly, many of the exercises can be given to students to do as homework or self-study work. The writing tasks in Section I at the end of each Unit are meant to be alternatives, from which the student or the teacher chooses the most interesting or most appropriate. Students on intensive courses may, of course, have the time to do more than one of the tasks.

The Units of the course vary slightly in length and level of difficulty, becoming progressively longer and more difficult through the book. Because of this, and the obvious variation in classroom situations, it is not possible to specify how much class time would be needed to complete a Unit. But, as an approximate guide, each Unit should provide enough work for three to four lessons, plus a written homework assignment.

The following notes explain the function of each type of exercise:

A Text
(and/or visual material)

This gives students a model for written work, along with facts or opinions they can use. Where possible, this should be prepared by students in advance, and re-read in class in connection with Sections B and C.

B Vocabulary

The explanations given here should be adequate for most Intermediate students, although other students may need further preparation. In the classroom situation, students should be encouraged to help each other with unfamiliar items, and the teacher should try to elicit explanations from the class before explaining anything himself.

C Comprehension

These are designed to be used as oral checks on students' understanding of the main points of the text, and can be supplemented by the teacher's own questions, whether more difficult or more simple, to suit the level of the class. If time is limited, these questions can be set along with the text as a preparatory homework. When used in class, students should ask each other, and also perhaps formulate their own questions, to reduce the amount of time spent listening to the teacher.

D Analysis

These questions are designed to develop students' skill at extracting information from the text or visual, at a more detailed level than normally dealt with by comprehension questions. They can be answered orally in class, or in writing.

E Inference

The purpose of these questions is to train the students to infer information from the context of the text or visual, without relying only on the explicitly stated information. So students are encouraged to speculate or hypothesise as to meanings 'behind' the text.

F Discussion

These questions give the students opportunity to discuss the wider implications of ideas or information in the text, thus preparing them for the written exercises where they will need a wider knowledge and understanding of the topic area they are writing about. The questions should be dealt with orally, and the teacher should decide how far the discussion element of the Unit should be developed. The main consideration here will be the extent to which students need further preparation of the factual content of their written work.

G Language Practice

The exercises under this heading give practice in the various structural and functional aspects of language that students will need to use in their writing exercises. Examples of the same forms also occur in the various textual models that are given, and the teacher should draw the students' attention to the way these forms are used. The exercises are designed primarily for oral work, but could of course be given as written practice. The exercises are all keyed at the back of the book.

H Writing Practice

In this section are a variety of exercises such as *Linking sentences*, *Sequencing*, *Reporting*, *Summarising* etc which give the students models and practice exercises covering areas of writing skill that students need to do the written tasks at the end of each Unit. This section prepares students for the specific forms and techniques used in writing, and draws attention to the differences between spoken and written English forms. The texts and other stimuli used as models in this section supplement the main text(s) used in Section A of each unit, giving examples of the same language constructions used in a wider variety of situations.

I Writing Task(s)

The tasks given are designed to practise the language and writing techniques that students have learned and developed through working with the Unit. The tasks are meant to be alternatives, and the teacher should decide which would be most suitable for his students, in terms of level of difficulty and degree of creative imagination required by the task. Students can of course attempt more than one task if sufficient time is available.

It will be noticed that the explanations and instructions in the Units are directed at the students, suggesting how they should approach the material. This is not meant to replace the teacher's guidance, although some students may wish to study the course on their own. This technique also gives students practice in understanding instructions, and allows the teacher to set certain tasks for homework or private study without having to laboriously explain the nature of each exercise.

1 Informal letters

A Text

> 24 Hills Rd,
> Cambridge,
> November 27th,
>
> Dear Sally,
>   Thanks for your letter. It seems ages since I saw you last - lovely to hear from you.
>   Glad you're enjoying yourself at college. Your new course sounds very interesting - but too much like hard work for me.
>   I've had enough hard work moving into the new flat (new address above). I've repainted most of it, and put up new pictures etc. Now I'm saving up for new furniture to match the paint!
>   Hope you can drop in when you're home on holiday. Give me a ring when you come back
>   All the best
>   Yours,
>   Andy.

B Vocabulary

ages	=	a long time
saving up	=	saving my money
to match	=	to suit; to look good with the colour of the paint
drop in	=	visit, come round to the house
give me a ring	=	telephone me
all the best	=	best wishes

C Comprehension

1 Who lives in Cambridge?
2 Where is Sally?
3 What has Andy just done?
4 What is he going to do soon?
5 What does Andy want Sally to do?

D Analysis

1 How does Andy know that Sally is doing a new course?
2 Are Andy and Sally friends, relatives, or lovers? Is it possible to say?
3 Where does Sally's family live? Is it possible to find out?

E Discussion

1 Why do people write letters to each other? What is the difference between a letter and a telephone call?
2 Do you prefer to write to people or to telephone them? Why?
3 This letter is hand written. A lot of letters are type written.

   Is there any difference between them in your opinion? Do you think one sort is more interesting or more friendly? Why?

G Writing Practice

1 Being informal (see also Unit 2)

When we are speaking or writing to people we know well, we use informal language. Sometimes we shorten words, or use different words. Look at the first sentence of the text:

> Thanks for your letter. It seems ages since I saw you.

In a formal letter this would be:

> Thank you for your letter. It seems a long time since we met.

So, *thanks* and *ages* are more informal or friendly. Using this list of formal and informal words, re-write the formal letter below, making it more friendly. (David Johnson is writing to Simon Hawkes.)

Formal:	Informal/friendly:
proposition	suggestion
thank you	thanks
opportunity	chance
yours sincerely	yours
I would like to	I'd like to
visit us	drop in
telephone me	give me a
if you are in	ring if you're
the area	passing

F Language Practice

1 Contractions

When we speak or write to friends, or speak quickly, some words become shorter, or disappear completely. Look at this example from the text:

> It is lovely to hear from you.
> LOVELY TO HEAR FROM YOU.

Now shorten these sentences in the same way:*
   a I am glad you're enjoying yourself.
   b I hope you can drop in.
   c I have been working hard this week.
   d Have you got any money?
   e Would you like a cigarette?

2 Here is an example of a different sort of contraction:

> I have had enough hard work.
> I'VE HAD ENOUGH HARD WORK.

Shorten the has/have/am/are/not words in the same way:*
   a I am saving my money.
   b She has bought a new car.
   c They could not help me.
   d We are going to America for the summer.
   e They have painted their house.

Dear Mr. Hawkes,

Thank you for your letter. I was very pleased to hear from you, as it is a long time since we last met. I hope you are well. I would like to have an opportunity to talk about your business proposition. Please telephone me, or visit us if you are in the area.

Yours sincerely,

David Johnson

David Johnson

2 Letter forms

Look again at the text in Section A. Look at the shape of the letter:

| address |

| date |

| opening greeting |

| (letter) |

| closing greeting |

| signature |

Practise using this shape. Write a letter to your parents, just writing your address, the date, and the greetings — leave the letter out!

3 Parts of a letter

Informal letters have different parts, with different phrases for different things. Here are some examples:

a Thanking the letter-writer
  – Thanks for your letter.
  – It was nice to hear from you.
  – I was glad to hear from you.

b Asking about health etc
  – How are you?
  – I hope you're well.
  – How's your job?

c Giving news
  – I've just got a new car.
  – I finally passed my exams!

d Making suggestions/invitations
  – Why don't you come for the weekend?

H Writing Tasks

1 Write a letter to an old friend you haven't seen for over a year. Use the letter plan and letter parts above, and invite your friend to visit you. (80-100 words)

2 Here is a letter your parents' English friends have written to you. Write a reply to them. Don't forget to answer all their questions. (100-120 words)

3 Your aunt has sent you a nice present for your birthday. Write a letter back to her, thanking her for it. Arrange a time when you can go and see her. (80—100 words)

34, Sheffield Rd,
Banchester,
April 24th

Dear Paul,

We have just had a letter from your parents, but we haven't heard from you for a long time. How are you? What are you doing now? Have you finished your exams? We hope you will be able to find a good job – it's very difficult sometimes.

We've just bought a new car, very fast, so we can take you sight-seeing when you come and see us. When are you going to stay for a holiday? Let us know and we'll meet you at the airport.

All the best,

Yours,

John and Sheila

2 Giving information

A Text

SPEND THE SUMMER IN BRITAIN!

HOLIDAY ENGLISH LTD

We specialise in English Language Holidays for young people, because they have special needs and interests - and our holiday courses are organised just for those interests:

* a special teaching programme that doesn't repeat the lessons you had at home, but builds on what you have learned and extends your English.

* a special social programme that makes sure you meet a lot of people to practise your English on - with lots of sport, excursions, theatre trips etc.

* special teachers and social organisers on duty all day, every day, to make your holiday enjoyable and useful.

* specially chosen families to live with, so you find out how English people really live.

Students coming to our schools and centres in Britain have included in their course fee:

Language classes - 3 academic hours per weekday in groups of maximum 15, according to standard of English.
Accommodation including all meals with carefully chosen families.

Our social organisers are always ready to help with advice on leisure activities and our hospitality secretaries with any accommodation problems.

INTERESTED?

Fill in the application form now, or write for further details to:

Holiday English Ltd
2-6 Church Street
Seabourne

B Vocabulary

accommodation = somewhere to stay
hospitality   = friendly attention to guests
fee   = price

C Comprehension

1 How many hours of English will you get in a week, if you go on this course?
2 Where will you live if you go on this course?
3 How many meals are included in the price?
4 What sort of people work for Holiday English, apart from the teachers?
5 What does a hospitality secretary do?

D Analysis

1 What is an academic hour? Can it mean more than one thing?
2 What opinion does Holiday English have about the other language schools in England?
3 Why does the brochure stress that the maximum number of students in a class is 15?

E Inference

1 What does this course offer that other courses do not?
  Why does this company think they are better than the other English language schools?
2 The brochure mentions 'accommodation problems'. What do you think they mean by this?

F Discussion

1 Why do many people go to England for summer courses? Is it in order to learn English, or to have a holiday?
2 If you went on this course, what would you expect to do, to see, to learn? What people would you meet?
3 Would you prefer to stay in a hotel, or with a family? What difference would this make to your holiday?

G Language Practice

1 Expressing your preferences

Here is an example of the way you can explain that you prefer doing one thing:
    swim – go riding
    I ENJOY SWIMMING, BUT I PREFER TO GO RIDING.
Make sentences from these words in the same way:*
    a listen to records / go to a concert
    b watch TV / go out
    c go to a football match / play football
    d eat meat / live on vegetarian food
    e have a bath / take a shower

2 Unfinished actions

If you started to do something in the past, and you're still doing it, then you can use the HAVE BEEN DOING form. Look at this example:
    I started to study English three years ago.
    I HAVE BEEN STUDYING ENGLISH FOR THREE YEARS.
Now change these sentences in the same way:*
    a I started to learn Spanish two years ago.
    b John started to live in London twenty years ago.
    c We started to attend this school ten days ago.
    d I started to stay here in Bournemouth a week ago.
    e Sally started to play the guitar a year ago.

H Writing Practice

1 Giving information

Here is the application form for a summer course in England. Fill in the information (or copy the form down, then fill it in). If you don't have any health or diet problems, imagine what problems other people might have.

Family Name.............................. Forename ....

Male or female................................Date of Birth..

Home Address ....

....Telephone number...

School Address...

Nationality..Passport No...

I have been learning English for.........................years

Name of School/Centre I wish to attend..

Dates From......................................To...

Please give any accommodation requirements...

....

Please give any special diet requirements..

....

Are you in good health? Please state any illness you may suffer from such as asthma etc.

....

In the event of illness or accident I should like the school to inform:

Name ....Address ....

....Telephone number ....

Signature of parent or guardian ....

Date ....

Profession or occupation of father ....

2 Expressing preferences

You have sent this application form to Holiday English Ltd, but they want some more information from you. They want to know what you would prefer to do. This is the letter they have written to you:

2-6 Church St.,
Seabourne,
England.

23rd April

Dear Miss Fernandez,

Thank you for sending us your application form. We have reserved a place for you on the summer course, amd now we need to know a little more about you. What sports are you interested in? Do you like to go to the cinema or the theatre? Would you like to go on excursions to historical places, or would you prefer to sunbathe on the beach? Can you sing or play a musical instrument? We are hoping to organise a concert one evening - would you like to join in?

Please let us know which activities you prefer, and whether you have any other interests or hobbies.

We look forward to meeting you,

Yours sincerely,

Holiday English Ltd.

You want to write back to give them the information they have asked for. Here is part of the letter you should write—fill in the gaps yourself.

(Write your address here)

Dear Holiday English,

Thank you for your letter of 23rd April. I am glad you have reserved my place on the........, I am looking forward to it. I am interested in sport, and my favourite is......... I also enjoy going to......... Although I like........, I would prefer to........ when there are no English lessons. I am also very interested in the concert evening - I could........ My other hobbies are........ and I hope that when I am in England I will be able to........

I look forward to.........

Yours........,

(Write your name here)

15

3 Being formal (see Unit 1)

When you are writing to someone you do not know, you need to use more formal English than when you are speaking or writing to a friend. For example, to a friend you might write:

See you soon!

But in a formal letter you would write:

I look forward to seeing you.

Here are some more examples:

Friendly:	Formal:
Thanks for your letter.	Thank you for your letter.
I'd like to. . .	I would like to. . .
How about going to the theatre?	Would you like to go to the theatre?
Can I borrow your car?	Would it be possible to borrow your car?

Now use these formal phrases to re-write this letter. Imagine you are writing to someone you don't know well – it must be more formal. The person's name is Christopher Harris.

Dear Chris,
　　Thanks for your letter ! I'd like to come to see you next weekend. Is that okay ? How about going to see a play on Saturday evening ? If the weather is fine, I'd like to go walking in the country — can I borrow some boots and a jacket ?
See you soon,
Yours,

(your name here)

I Writing Tasks

1 The school has found you a place in a family. Write a formal letter to the family, explaining who you are, what your interests are, and what you want to do on your holiday.

2 At the end of the course you want to tell the course organisers what you thought of the course. Write a formal letter telling them what was good and bad, what you did, and what you preferred doing.

3 A friend of yours is starting his own summer course, and wants you to write the publicity material for him. Look at Section A again, and write your own publicity brochure.

4 You are applying for a place at University, to study English. Write a formal letter giving information about yourself, your interests, how good your English is, and what job you want to do.

3 Describing people

A Text

Robert Zimmerman was born in North Hibbing, a small mining town in the USA, in 1941. At school he dreamed of becoming a rock and roll singer, and taught himself to play the guitar. He changed his mind, however, when he heard the music of Woody Guthrie, a well-known folk singer. He then started writing his own songs, and took them to the CBS record company in New York, telling them his name was Bob Dylan. His first record was produced in 1962, and made him famous almost overnight.

What was it that made this pale thin young man into a world famous star at the age of 21? It certainly wasn't his voice, which even his fans found hard and aggressive. The answer lay in the songs he sang – songs which he had written himself. Unlike most pop songs of the time, Dylan's songs had something to say about the world, and about people. Songs like *Blowin' in the Wind* and *The Times they are a-Changin* criticised the ideas of the older generation, especially the wars which they had been involved in. With his long, untidy hair and his scruffy clothes, Dylan was a symbol of rebellion for the younger generation. He symbolised their rejection of the ideas and morality of their parents.

Dylan made a series of successful records until 1966, when the famous *Blonde on Blonde* was produced. Soon after, though, he had a serious motorcycle accident, and 'disappeared' for two years, living a quiet life with his wife and children. When he finally produced a new LP in 1968, his fans were shocked by the change in style – the music was much softer, and the songs were not so critical.

Many fans of Dylan were disappointed by this LP (*John Wesley Harding*) and also by the records that followed over the next few years – *Nashville Skyline*, *Self-portrait*, *New Morning* and *Planet Waves*. There were some good songs on all of these, but many people felt he had lost the power to write songs with a message, songs that you could think about. It was only with the production of *Blood on the tracks* in 1975 that Dylan seemed to return to the creativity of *Blonde on Blonde*, almost ten years before. In the same year he produced the LP *Desire*, which was his first really successful record in a long time, and also started to give concerts again, supported by a large electric band. It was in the same year that Dylan's wife left him, and this might have influenced him to work harder. In fact, some people believe that it was his unhappiness at this time that helped him to write better songs. This unhappiness can also be seen in Dylan's first film, *Renaldo and Clara*, which was produced in 1978, and which describes both his life as a singer and also his relationship with his wife. It is typical of Dylan's rejection of 'normal' ideas that the film was 4½ hours long!

Fans of Dylan have got used to his changes of style, from folk singer to rock group leader to film producer. But the biggest surprise came in 1979, when he announced that he had been 'born again' and was now a serious Christian. There is no doubt that he will continue to change and surprise his audiences.

B Vocabulary

fans	= supporters; people who like an artist/sport
scruffy	= untidy, not smart
rebellion	= a fight against established ideas/ politics
band	= group of musicians
to announce	= to say something publicly

C Comprehension

1 When did Bob Dylan first become famous?
2 How old was he at this time?
3 What was his real name?
4 When did he become interested in folk singing?
5 Why did he disappear for two years?

D Analysis

1 What made Dylan different from singers before him?
2 What made his songs so popular? What does the text suggest?
3 Read the text again and write down the words and phrases used to describe Dylan. Analyse them into two groups:
   a what he is like (appearance, personality)
   b what he has done

E Inference

1 What ideas of the older generation' do you think Dylan and his fans were rejecting?
2 Why do you think some people linked the fact that Dylan's wife left him with the fact that his songs became better?

F Discussion

1 Dylan's records are bought by people who do not understand much English. Why do you think this is true?
2 Dylan, like many other singers, has sold millions of records all over the world. Why do you think pop or rock music has become so popular?

G Language Practice

It is not interesting to describe people with only one word, such as
   He is clever.
To make our meaning more clear, and more interesting, we use qualifying words which make the first word stronger or weaker:
   He is very clever (stronger).
   He is quite clever (weaker).

Here is a scale of qualifying words, from strong to weak:
1 She's extremely intelligent.
2 She's very intelligent.
3 She's rather intelligent.
4 She's intelligent.
5 She's quite intelligent.
6 She's not stupid.

Now complete these sentences, choosing one of the qualifying words, or deciding not to use one, depending on the sense of the sentence. Remember, if you want to use type 6, you will change the word given into its opposite – e.g. (clever) could become 'not stupid'.*

a That was a (interesting) film – the best I've seen this year.
b The new British Leyland car is good value for money, but it's certainly (expensive).
c Despite criticism from the newspapers, the Prime Minister's speech was (popular) with businessmen.
d The actors' performance was (good) for the first night of the production.
e He's (clever), but not clever enough to become a professor.
f I was surprised when I met the director – he's (young).

H Writing Practice

1 Describing words

There are different sorts of words for different sorts of description. Find out what this list of words means, and try to fit the words into the groups in this table. You must decide if each word is positive or negative, and if it describes physical or personality details.

	positive	negative
physical description		
personality description		
description of work done		

Word-list: successful, sensitive, smart, tall, ugly, famous, scruffy, unoriginal, arrogant, generous, inefficient, aggressive

2 Describing faces

Look at these people. Write a short description of
each face, including physical details and suggestions about the personality of the face:

3 Biography

A biography is a description of what a person has done in his or her life. Here is an example of an actor's short biography:

John Golding first acted at school, and then went to Drama School in London. His first big success was in Macbeth, at the age of 25. He has become famous by appearing in the television programme *Target*, about a London detective. He also sings his own songs.

Now write a similar short biography for these two actors:

a Susie Wyatt /youth club/university/amateur plays in Oxford/ BBC radio 1975/ famous in TV advertisement for tobacco/ also American films

b Sir David Lawrence /1903/ church festivals/ drama school/ early films in Hollywood/ famous in TV version of Shakespeare/ also photographer

I Writing Tasks

1 You are meeting some friends of your parents at the airport, but they don't know what you look like. Write a short note describing yourself and your appearance. (50-80 words)

2 Your best friend is trying to get a very good job, and asks you to write a reference for her. Write a description of her personality and how she works, and explain why she should get the job of Sales Manager. (100-120 words)

3 You are the Public Relations Officer for a big record company. You want to make a young pop singer very famous, but no-one has heard of him. Write a press release which will explain to all the newspapers etc why this new singer is very important. (50-80 words) All you know about him is:

Name — Chris Callan
Age — 23
Weight — 14st (89 kg)
Height — 6ft 5 ins
Hair — black
Type of song — fast, loud music

4 Here are some facts about Muhammad Ali. Use these, and any other information you can find about him, to write a short biography of the famous boxer. Add your own opinions to the facts, as in the text at the beginning of the Unit:

Born Louisville 1942, won first fight 1959, given contract 1960, became Muslim 1964, got divorced 1966, 1967 refused to join Army — lost boxing licence, 1970 got licence back; 1974 won title of World Champion back again from George Foreman; 1978 lost title to Leon Spinks; now millionaire; retired from sport. (100-120 words)

4 Describing places/objects

A Text

FOR SALE

For Sale

A beautiful 4 bedroomed house, built in 1979, on St Andrews Avenue. The house stands on its own in the middle of trees and open space, away from the road. There is a large garden with a beautiful lawn and flower-beds. The house is only about 1 mile from the centre of the town, which has a large shopping centre, cinemas, a theatre and so on. The railway station is also very close.

The house is heated by gas central heating. There are four bedrooms, and a bathroom. The biggest bedroom also has a second bathroom en suite. Downstairs there is a dining room and a very large living room. The kitchen is next to the dining room, and there are cupboards and equipment already fitted. From the front door, the visitor comes into a lobby, with a cloakroom to the right. Then, on the right of the stairs is the boiler room. The hall leads into the kitchen. The house is very well-decorated and painted. There is also a garage.

Cost: £35000

Further information from   Hazletts Estate Agents

B Vocabulary

on its own = alone
en suite = it is connected directly to the bedroom with a door
equipment = machines which do a particular job; eg washing machine
boiler = a machine which heats water for a central heating system
cloakroom = a room to put coats in, especially visitors' coats

C Comprehension

1 What is the house surrounded by?
2 How far is it from the town?
3 Where is the cloakroom?
4 Which bedroom has its own bathroom?
5 What is used to heat the house?

D Analysis

1 Here is a plan of the house, but the names of the rooms are missing. Read the text again, and write in the names of the rooms in the correct place:

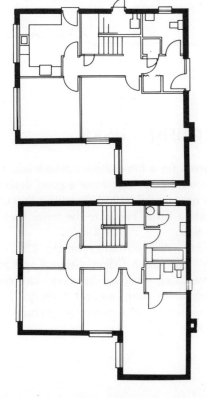

E Inference

1 The house is not quite new, so someone has lived here, and is moving out of the house. Does this mean that there is something wrong with the house? What reason could there be?
2 The information in the text is for people who want to buy the house. Why is information about the railway station included? Surely the people in the town know where it is?

F Discussion

1 In Britain, half the houses are owned by the people who live in them. In other countries, most people rent their houses. What are the advantages of each system?
2 Some people prefer to live in a house, with a garden, a long way from the city. Others like to live in flats, in the middle of the city. What are the good and bad points of each way of living?

G Language Practice

Describing
When we are describing, we can say either:
 The house has four bedrooms. *Or*
 There are four bedrooms in the house.
The second sentence is a little more formal, and is useful if you are describing a list of things. Now make sentences like the second one from these:*
a The house has two bathrooms, both upstairs.
b The garden has a very large lawn.
c The town has a good shopping centre and two cinemas.
d The hall has a cloakroom to the right.
e The kitchen has a lot of fitted cupboards.

H Writing Practice

1 Expanding descriptions

The text is a long description of a house. The estate agent wrote this after making notes – he expanded the notes into a description:

Notes
big garden/lawn/ flowers

Description
There is a large garden with a beautiful lawn and flowerbeds

In the same way, use these notes to write a description of a flat you want to sell:

Notes

2 bedroom/3rd floor/balcony/south/central heating

town centre/10 mins. walk from station/ lift / bathroom /shower/ kitchen /washing machine / living room/thick carpet

2 Exaggerating

Sometimes people exaggerate in descriptions – they say something is better than it really is. For example:

Normal	*Exaggerated*
a nice house	a wonderful house
a pleasant garden	a delightful garden
good value for money	outstanding value for money
a comfortable chair	a superbly comfortable chair
this is a fast car	this is a very powerful car

Re-write this description of a stereo record player, and exaggerate it. Use the words above, and any other exaggerated words you know:

This is a good record player, with a nice design. It is good value for money, and has some special features. As well as loudspeakers, there are headphones which are comfortable to wear. The equipment produces good sound, with a lot of power. We suggest you listen to it when you have time.

3 Advertisements

The small advertisements in newspapers use a lot of words which are shorter than usual:

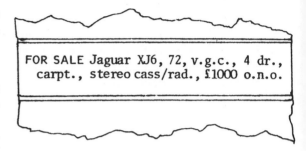

FOR SALE Jaguar XJ6, 72, v.g.c., 4 dr., carpt., stereo cass/rad., £1000 o.n.o.

This means:

For sale – a Jaguar XJ6 type which was new in 1972. It is in very good condition. It is a four-door model, and has a carpet and stereo cassette and radio fitted. The price is £1000 or the nearest offer.

Now re-write this advertisement as a description:

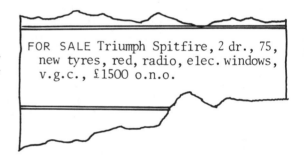

FOR SALE Triumph Spitfire, 2 dr., 75, new tyres, red, radio, elec. windows, v.g.c., £1500 o.n.o.

I Writing Tasks

1 You work for a big company which sells colour televisions. You must write a good description of the new model. (100-150 words) You can exaggerate a little. Here are the notes they have given you:

MS345 – new portable – weighs 12kg – small size – big screen (35cm) – sound and picture immediately – big loudspeaker – can connect headphones – can use car battery – 2 years guarantee – clear colours in picture – cheap (£200)

2 The city where you live wants to bring more tourists to the area. Write a description of the city, its sights, what you can do and see there, to make it interesting for tourists. This will go into the tourist guide — so write to the tourists and use *you*. (150-200 words)

3 Your friend wants to rent a house, and is looking at advertisements. He shows you one which he cannot understand. Write it out as a description so that it is easy to understand (50-80 words). You will need to guess some of the abbreviations.

ACCOMMODATION TO LET: furnished house, 2 bed., bthrm. with shower, sep.wc., kitch. with fitted cupbd., good decor., gas c/htg., 15 mins. t. centre. £25 per wk.

5 Describing the past

A Text

The Olympic Games

Everyone has seen the Olympic Games at some time – either in Mexico, Montreal or Moscow. And everyone knows that the Greeks started the Games. But most people are unaware of the real story.

The original Olympics took place nearly 3000 years ago, in the year 776 BC. Many different sports were played, including boxing, running, throwing the discus, though there were fewer sports involved than in the modern Olympics. People came from all over Greece to watch the Games beneath Mount Olympus, and even cities or states that were fighting wars stopped them for the duration of the games.

The Games were held every five years, until they were banned by the Romans in AD 393. They continued for such a long time because people believed in the philosophy behind the Olympics: the idea that a healthy body produced a healthy mind, and that the spirit of competition in sport and games was preferable to the competition that caused wars.

After the Romans stopped the Olympics, the concept was lost for nearly 1500 years, until in 1894 Baron Pierre de Coubertin had an idea. He thought it would be possible to start the Games again, inviting sportsmen from different countries, to create a spirit of peace and healthy competition. Many others felt this was worthwhile, and on April 6, 1896 the first new Olympics were held in Greece. Only 50,000 people saw these Games, but the rest of the world soon became enthusiastic, and from 1900 the Games were held every four years in a different country. Only three Olympics were cancelled because of war – 1916, 1940, and 1944. In Tokyo in 1964 they reached their peak in terms of size – there were over 5700 competitors from 94 countries.

B Vocabulary

unaware of	=	not knowing the facts
duration	=	the period of time from beginning to end
spirit	=	feeling, idea
competition	=	taking part in a game or sport, and wanting to win
worthwhile	=	worth doing; the effort would not be wasted
peak	=	highest point

C Comprehension

1 Who started the Olympic Games?
2 What was the reason behind the Games?
3 How were the 'new' Olympics different?
4 Why did some Olympics not take place?
5 Why are the Games called the Olympic Games?

E Inference

In the original Olympic Games, people stopped fighting wars to take part. In 1916, 1940 and 1944 this did not happen. What do you think was the difference?

F Discussion

1 Why is sport so popular? What makes it so interesting?
2 Many people do not play sport, but love to watch it.
   Why do you think these people prefer watching to playing?

G Language Practice

1 Describing the past

The usual way of describing the past is with sentences like: 'The Greeks started the Olympic Games'. But if we want to stress the action, and not the person who did it, we use the form:
   The Olympic Games were started by the Greeks.

Now change these descriptions of the Games in the same way:*
a The Romans stopped the Games in 393.
b The sportsmen played many different games.
c Fifty thousand people saw the Games in 1896.
d The organisers cancelled the Games in 1916.

2 Describing changes

When something has changed, we can describe the situation in the past in this way:
   He used to live in London (but he doesn't now).

Describe these changes in the same way:*
a People watched the Games beneath Mount Olympus (but not now).
b The Greeks stopped their wars to go to the Games.
c Women were not allowed to join in the Games.
d They held Olympics every five years.

H Writing Practice

1 Sequencing

When describing the past, it is important to get everything in the right order. This description of the life of the writer Ernest Hemingway is in the wrong order. Re-write it in the correct sequence, and put the dates on the left:

   wounded in Austria 1918
   shot himself in Idaho, USA 1961
   won Nobel Prize for *The Old Man and the Sea*
   first book published 1925
   born 1898
   lived in Cuba just before Second World War
   published *The Old Man and the Sea* 1952
   won medal for getting wounded
   worked as journalist in Second World War

3 Punctuation

To make descriptions (or any text) more easy to understand, it is important to use full stops and commas to break the sentences up. The full stop always comes at the end. The comma gives a break in the sentence, like that, to separate one idea from another. Some words like *however* or *of course* usually have commas on both sides. This text has lost its commas and full stops – re-write it and put them back.

every time you post a letter it is carried by the Royal Mail during the Middle Ages the Royal Posts were only for state business monks scholars and merchants made their own arrangements for sending letters in Tudor times however the Royal Mail service overseas began to carry private letters in fact after 1609 all post for places in this country had to be carried by the Royal Mail

Note Don't forget to write capital letters for the first word of each sentence.

I Writing Tasks

1 You have applied for a job as a hotel manager, and you must write a description of your life so far – age, education, what jobs you have done etc. Write a description – it doesn't need to be true. (120-150 words)

2 Here are some notes on the history of football. Use them to write a description of how it has changed and developed (120-150 words):

3 Write a description of a disaster you have seen or experienced or heard about. Describe what happened, when it was, what you saw, how it ended – examples: a car accident/plane crash/earthquake/fire. (120-150 words)

4 Find out as much as you can about a well-known person (actor, politician, pop star etc) that you find interesting, and write a description of their life and what they have done in it. (120-150 words)

Game played for centuries/big teams / no rules
people often killed/ King Henry tried to ban it (1410)
first organised in Football League 1888
arguments about rules/ two games - Soccer and
Rugby Football
other countries learned game/World Cup started 1930/
England joined in 1950
players now very rich
people worried about violence in field / English fans
also violent
still most popular sport in world

5 The series of pictures below show what happened on one of the Apollo moon landings. Use the pictures to write a description of the journey and landing. (100-150 words)

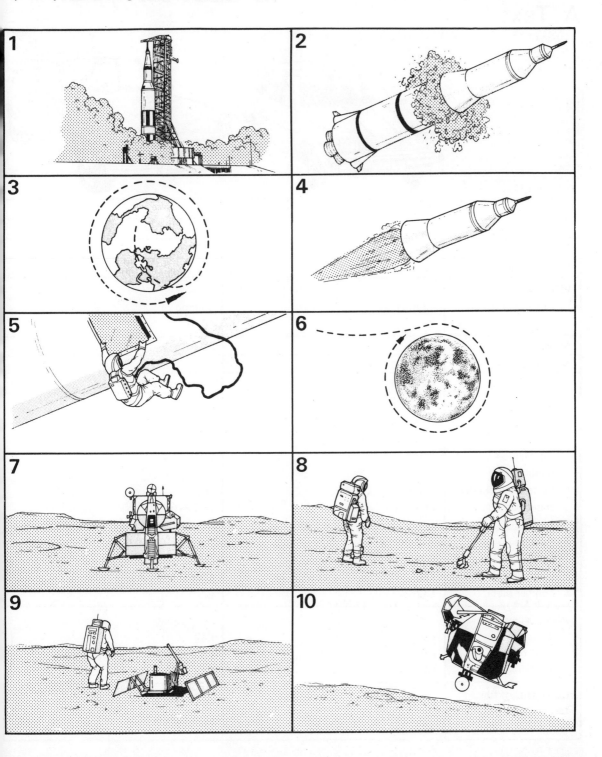

6 Comparing

A Text

Name	Coral	Bella
Country of origin	Japan	Britain
Price	£3500	£4100
Maximum speed	98 mph	102 mph
Petrol consumption		
a miles per gallon	32 mpg	28 mpg
b litres per 100 km	8.71	10.01
Number of doors	5	3
Number of seats	5	5
Type of steering	standard	power-assisted
Special features:		
reclining seats	fitted	fitted
carpets	fitted	£100 extra
cigar lighter	fitted	not fitted
double brake system	not fitted	fitted
heated rear window	£35 extra	fitted
stereo radio	£69 extra	£83 extra
Extra costs:		
delivery	£60	£85
seat belts	£50	£80
number plate	£12	£7
Cost of spare parts		
bumper	£35	£17
set of brakes	£11	£9
windscreen	£41	31
Comments of the test driver:	Smooth to drive, but a little noisy	Quiet and safe, but not very comfortable

B Vocabulary

country of origin = country the car comes from
petrol consumption = the amount of petrol used
reclining seats = seats that can move to let you lie down
bumper = the long piece of metal at the front of a car, which protects it
power-assisted = helped by the power of the engine

C Comprehension

1 Which car is the cheapest?
2 Which car has the cheapest spare parts?
3 Which car always has a double brake system?
4 Why is there a difference in the number of doors?
5 What did the test driver think was bad about each car?

D Analysis

1 If you take the total cost of each car, including price, extra costs, and the cost of special features, which is the cheapest car?
2 If you take a set of spare parts for each car, and work out how much petrol each car would use in 100,000 km of driving – which is the cheapest car?

E Inference

The spare parts of the cheaper car are more expensive than those of the expensive car. This seems crazy – what could be the explanation of this?

F Language Practice

1 Comparing

Here are some of the sentences we use when comparing two things – for example, the two cars in the text:

The Coral *is longer than* the Bella.
The Bella is *not as long as* the Coral.
The Coral has carpets included in the price, *whereas* the carpets in the Bella cost extra.
Although the Coral is cheaper, the spare parts are more expensive.

Now practise writing sentences like this, also about the two cars.*

2 Connecting

Here are two ways to connect short sentences in comparisons:
a The Rolls Royce is the most expensive car made in Britain.
It is the most reliable car.
NOT ONLY IS THE ROLLS ROYCE THE MOST EXPENSIVE CAR MADE IN BRITAIN, IT IS THE MOST RELIABLE AS WELL.
b The Mini is very cheap and reliable.
There is not much room inside.
ON THE ONE HAND THE MINI IS VERY CHEAP AND RELIABLE, BUT ON THE OTHER HAND THERE IS NOT MUCH ROOM INSIDE.

Now write sentences comparing the two cars in the text, using the same sentence forms.*

3 American vocabulary

The names of the parts of a car are different in America:

UK	USA
bumper	fender
bonnet	hood
boot	trunk
windscreen	windshield
tyre	tire
saloon car	sedan
puncture	flat

Practise using these by re-writing this text in American English:

The new Pronto saloon is really well-built, with special steel bumpers and a laminated windscreen. To stop glare, the bonnet is painted black. The boot is large and wide, with space for several suitcases as well as the spare tyre in case of punctures.

G Discussion

1 The text comparing the two cars mentions a lot of information. Which do you think are the most important pieces of information when buying a car?
2 Which of these cars would you choose, if you had the money to buy one? Give your reasons.

H Writing Practice

1 Recommending

When we recommend a product or a restaurant to a friend we usually explain:
a why it's good
b why it's better than the others
Here are some examples of explanations:
a I like this restaurant *because of* the atmosphere.
It's a good theatre *because it's got* a bar.
The best thing about this car is the speed.
b *It's better than* the shop next door *because of* the service.

Now write a short recommendation for each of the following, using the information given:
Alfi's restaurant – good food/continental chef/ soft lights/reasonable prices
Barbara's hair salon – latest styles/ free coffee/ loud music/ friendly staff
The new Rolling Stones LP – interesting cover/ more songs than before/better quality sound than before/more instruments used
Use the sentence forms above, and start with
I'd recommend. . .

2 Complaining

If you buy something that is not as good as it should be, you can complain. You compare what you expected with what you actually got:
This digital watch *is supposed to* give the date—but it doesn't.
These shoes only lasted two months—ten months *less than you claimed.*
The repairs on my car cost three times *more than you claimed* they would.

Using the same forms, complain about the problems you have had with this watch:

What it's supposed to do:	*In fact*
show 1/10th of a second	only seconds
have a light at night	not working
have an alarm bell	doesn't ring
be waterproof	stops under water
battery should last one year	lasted three months

I Writing Tasks

1 Make a table (like the text) of the good and bad points about going camping instead of going to a hotel for your holiday. Compare the different situations, and make a choice at the end.

2 You have bought a dishwashing machine, but it doesn't work in the way you expected. Write a letter to the manufacturer complaining about it. (80-100 words)

3 You have a friend who is going to buy a stereo music system. He wants to know whether to buy one for playing records only, or one for playing cassettes only. Which system would you recommend? What reasons would you give? (80-100 words)

Some ideas:

records	*cassettes*
can find one song quickly	play for a longer time
more information on cover	can record LPs free
cheaper to buy	can record radio programmes
better quality sound	easier to keep clean

4 Here are two mopeds:

The Maxi is French, the Flexi is Italian. Here is some information about them. You are comparing them for a magazine. Write a description of them, showing the good and bad points of each. (80-100 words)

Maxi
very heavy
fast on hills
uncomfortable
good brakes
double headlight
reliable
expensive

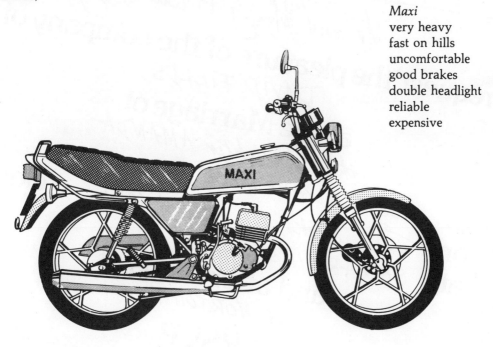

Flexi:
light
cheaper than average
bad to start
bad on hills
cheap spare parts
difficult to lock
comfortable to ride

You can make up extra information.

7 Invitations
A Text

Mr. and Mrs J. P. Bunberry

request the pleasure of the company of

DAVID FIELDS

at the Marriage of

their daughter AMANDA

to   ROGER DAVENPORT   at   12-15   o'clock

on   JULY 27th

at   St MARTIN'S

and afterwards at

THE NORTON HOTEL

RSVP

For those guests coming from outside the town, here are directions
for finding the church and the hotel:

Driving from London, leave the motorway and follow the signs for
the Town Centre until you come to a hospital on your left. Immediately after this is a T-junction, where you have to turn right -
it's a one-way system. Take the first left, then turn left again
by Woolworths. About 200 yards along on the right is a car park.
Park there, since there is no space outside the church. Opposite
the car park is a narrow street. Go down there, and turn right -
the church is at the bottom of the lane.

To reach the Norton Hotel, turn right out of the car park, then
left at the traffic lights. Drive about half a mile and turn left
at the T-junction. When you come to the roundabout, turn right,
and look for a Texaco garage on the left. Take the first road on
the right after the garage - the hotel is at the end of the road.

B Vocabulary

request = ask for (formal)
RSVP = please answer this invitation
directions = instructions for finding a place
T-junction = a crossroads shaped like the letter T
lane = a narrow road or street
roundabout = where several roads meet and make a circle

C Comprehension

1 Who is getting married to Amanda Burberry?
2 Look at this map. It shows the town where Amanda and Roger are getting married. Read the text again and work out the position of the church and the hotel on the map.

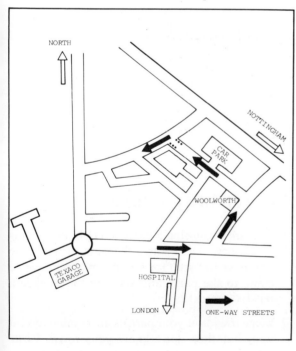

D Analysis

1 Why do you think the directions are given for people driving from London? What does this tell you about the guests?
2 Neither Amanda nor Roger live in this small town. Why do you think the wedding is here?

E Inference

The invitation refers to something happening at the Norton Hotel. What is it?

F Language Practice

1 Invitations

Look at the invitation in the text:

Mr and Mrs Burberry request the pleasure of the company of David Fields at the marriage of their daughter Amanda.

This is very formal, and would not be used except for special occasions such as weddings. Normally, when speaking or writing to people we know, we use sentences like:

Would you like to come to dinner?
How would you like to come to dinner tomorrow?
I'm having a party—would you like to come along?
How about coming to dinner tomorrow? (*informal*)

Now practise these sentences, by making invitations for these situations:*
a You are organising a picnic in the country.
b You are going to the sea for the weekend.
c You are going to the theatre on Friday.
d You are going for a meal and then to a discotheque.

2 Refusing an invitation

Accepting an invitation is very easy — you thank the person and say yes. Refusing is more difficult, because you need to give a reason. Here are some examples —

That's very kind of you, but I've already arranged something.
I'd love to come, but I've got to work.
Thanks all the same, but I'm afraid I'm meeting some friends.

Now use sentences like these to refuse the invitations you made in Section 1.*

G Writing Practice

1 Timetables

If you are arranging something, and your friend is not travelling by car, you will need to explain how to use buses or trains. Look at this bus timetable:

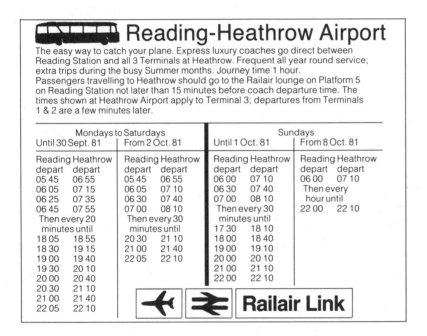

Reading-Heathrow Airport

The easy way to catch your plane. Express luxury coaches go direct between Reading Station and all 3 Terminals at Heathrow. Frequent all year round service; extra trips during the busy Summer months. Journey time 1 hour.
Passengers travelling to Heathrow should go to the Railair lounge on Platform 5 on Reading Station not later than 15 minutes before coach departure time. The times shown at Heathrow Airport apply to Terminal 3; departures from Terminals 1 & 2 are a few minutes later.

| Mondays to Saturdays | | Sundays | |
Until 30 Sept. 81	From 2 Oct. 81	Until 1 Oct. 81	From 8 Oct. 81
Reading Heathrow depart depart	Reading Heathrow depart depart	Reading Heathrow depart depart	Reading Heathrow depart depart
05 45 06 55	05 45 06 55	06 00 07 10	06 00 07 10
06 05 07 15	06 05 07 10	06 30 07 40	Then every
06 25 07 35	06 30 07 40	07 00 08 10	hour until
06 45 07 55	07 00 08 10	Then every 30	22 00 22 10
Then every 20	Then every 30	minutes until	
minutes until	minutes until	17 30 18 10	
18 05 18 55	20 30 21 10	18 00 18 40	
18 30 19 15	21 00 21 40	19 00 19 10	
19 00 19 40	22 05 22 10	20 00 20 10	
19 30 20 10		21 00 21 10	
20 00 20 40		22 00 22 10	
20 30 21 10			
21 00 21 40			
22 05 22 10			

✈ ≷ **Railair Link**

This bus takes people to and from Heathrow Airport. It takes one hour. Your friend wants to catch a plane at 12.15, and must be in the airport by 11.15. Write a note to tell him what bus he should get from Reading. He is going on a Saturday in November.

Tell him also what time he should be at Reading Station and where he should wait for the bus.

Here are some phrases to use:
In order to get to . . . by . . ., you should. . .
Take the . . . bus to . . .
You'll arrive at. . .

2 Giving directions

The text at the beginning of the Unit only gave directions for people driving from London. Look at the map again, and write the directions for people driving from the North. Remember to use these phrases from the text:
Turn left at. . .
Take the first left. . .
When you come to the . . ., turn right.

H Writing Tasks

1 You are organising a party to celebrate moving into a new flat. Write a letter to a friend who you have not seen for a year, and invite her to come to the party and stay for the weekend. (80-100 words)

2 Some friends of your parents are coming to visit you, but they don't know your town. Write them a letter, giving directions to find your house. (80-100 words)

3 You have received a letter inviting you to the wedding of someone you don't know very well. You can't go, and so you write a polite letter refusing the invitation. Make up your own reason for not going. (80-100 words)

4 One of your friends is studying in Manchester, and wants to come and visit you in London. He is coming on a Saturday, and you can't meet him until at least 18.00. Write a note to him suggesting which train he should get, and explain all the times etc he needs to know. Suggest a place to meet. (50-80 words)

Principal Services: Manchester, Stockport, Wilmslow, Macclesfield, Stoke-on-Trent → Watford, London

Weekdays

	Manchester Piccadilly	Stockport	Wilmslow	Macclesfield	Stoke-on-Trent	Watford Junction	London Euston
🛏	0027	0038	→	→	0123	→	0407
✕	0600a	0616a	0631a	→	0650c	0928p	0914
B● ✕	0700	0708u	→	0722u	0743	1031j	0934h
SX ✕			0657	→	→	1031g	0955a
SO ✕			0707	→	→	1031g	0955a
SX ●	0733	0741u	0748u	→	→	→	0958
● ✕	0738	0746u	→	0800u	0825	→	1015
✕	0810	0818u	0828u	→	→	1025s	1044
✕	0834	0842u	→	0856u	0917	→	1115
B ✕	0910	0918u	0928u	→	→	1231d	1200
B● ✕	0934	0942u	→	0956	1017	→	1214
🚋	0945	0956	1007	→	→	1331g	
B● ✕	1010	1018u	1028u	→	→	→	1249
✕	1110	1118u	→	1132	1153	→	1350
B ✕	1045	1056	1107	→	→	1431g	1359a
✕	1210	1218u	1228u	→	→	1531d	1500
✕	1310	1318u	→	1332	1353	→	1550
✕	1245	1256	1307	→	→	1631g	1604a
✕	1410	1418u	→	1432	1453	→	1650
✕			1407	→	→	→	1704a
B ✕	1510	1518u	1528u	→	→	1728s	1747
SX ✕	1550	1558u	→	1612u	1633	1807s	1827
SX ✕	1610	1618u	1628u	→	→	1829s	1849
SX ●	1700	→	1713u	→	→	1907s	1926
B ✕	1710	1718u	→	1736u	1753	1931s	1951
SX 🚋			1657	→	→	1941a	2001a
SO ✕			1707	→	→	2000a	2020a
● ✕	1810	1818u	1828u	1814k	1843k	2040s	2100
①			1907	→	→	2124a	2143a
✕	1910	1918u	→	1932	1953	2128s	2150
	2010	2018u	2028u	2014c	2043c	2240s	2259
🛏	2245	2256	2307	→	2309	→	0227m

Notes

a	Change at Crewe
b	Change at Stoke-on-Trent
c	Change at Stafford
d	Change at Rugby
g	Change at Crewe and Rugby
h	On Saturdays arrives **0939**
j	Saturdays only. Change at Rugby.
k	Monday to Fridays only. Change at Stafford
m	Change at Crewe and on Sunday mornings arrives 0307 🛏 Crewe to London
n	Change at Crewe. Until 7 September arrives 7 minutes earlier.
p	Change at Rugby. Saturdays arrives 0935
s	Stops to Set-down only
u	Stops to Pick-up only
B	✕ Mondays to Fridays, 🚋 Saturdays
C	✕ Mondays to Fridays only
SO	Saturdays only
SX	Saturdays excepted

8 Preferences and choices

A Text

My money and my life

JOHANNA YOUNGER is 15 and likes the Stranglers, John Travolta and art. She would like to be a film make-up artist when she leaves school, "If I can get my union-card ..."

"I used to get 80p a week pocket-money from my parents, but as that wasn't very much and I got bored on Saturdays I decided to get a job. Now I work in a baker's shop from half-past-twelve to half-past-five: I get £2.53 for that, 60p a week pocket-money and 40p every time I do baby-sitting. Usually I spend it on clothes, cosmetics, fares to go out to disco's or parties and to buy a bottle.

My parents haven't really got much money, but then they're not poor either. We get plenty of clothes and things — well, not plenty, but enough. We're just comfortable really; maybe we'd like a bit more to have a cleaner in. I'd like a certain standard of living when I leave home; a nice house, nice furniture and clothes. I suppose £80-£90 a week would be enough for me to live comfortably. I wouldn't like to be really well-off because then you stand more chance of being robbed or mugged."

B Vocabulary

The Stranglers	= an English punk-rock group
pocket-money	= spending money that some children get every week from their parents
cosmetics	= what women use to make up their faces
fares	= what you pay on buses or trains
buy a bottle	= here: to get a bottle of wine to take to a party
well-off	= rich
mugged	= attacked, beaten and robbed

C Comprehension

1 Does Johanna work full-time? What else does she do?
2 Why did she decide to get a weekend job?
3 What must she do before she can get a job as a make-up artist?
4 Why wouldn't Johanna want to be rich?
5 If her parents had a little more money, what would they spend it on?

D Analysis

1 Johanna says that she took a job because she was bored on Saturdays. Can you suggest any reasons for this boredom?
2 Why should Johanna need a union card before she can get a job in films? What reasons may there be?

E Discussion

1 Do you agree with Johanna that rich people are more likely to be mugged in the street – or is it only coincidence?
2 Johanna earns £2.53 for five hours work in the shop. This would be about £20 for a 40-hour week. Is it a fair wage or not? How does it compare with the amount she would like to have each week?

F Language Practice

1 Giving preferences

A simple way to show which of two things you prefer is to use:

I'd rather go swimming than riding.
I'd prefer to go to the theatre tonight. (= *one occasion*)
I prefer red wine to white wine. (= *in general*)

Now answer these questions using one of the forms:*
a Which car would you prefer to have – a Rolls or a Mercedes?
b Which do you prefer – white or brown bread?
c Would you rather be a politician or an artist?
d Would you prefer more money and less free time in your life, or more time and less money?

2 Contrasting

To contrast two things, such as two products you want to choose one of, you can use these sentences:

This car is cheap. That car is expensive.
THIS CAR IS CHEAP, WHEREAS THAT ONE IS EXPENSIVE.

If you want to contrast what someone has done with what you thought they would do, you can use this form:

That car was very old and rusty. Jane bought it.
ALTHOUGH THAT CAR WAS VERY OLD AND RUSTY, JANE BOUGHT IT.

Now make sentences contrasting these things or situations:*
a Cowboy films/interesting – love stories/boring
b Beethoven's music/good quality – pop music/rubbish
c Travelling by car/fast/expensive – walking/cheap/slow
d Jim had no money / went to Bali on holiday
e Alan very lazy at school/passed exams

G Writing Practice

Preferences

1 Look at the text again, and write a description of Johanna's preferences – what she prefers to do in her free time, what she would prefer to do in the future. use the sentences from the section above.

2 Here are some notes on two different colour televisions.
Write a description which contrasts the two, and say what you prefer about each one:

TV A	*TV B*
real wooden case	imitation wood
53 cm screen	65 cm screen
2 loudspeakers	1 loudspeaker
£299	£359

3 Choosing a job

There are many things to think about when choosing a job. For example:

wages?	outside, or in an office?
hours?	travelling the world?
length of holidays?	free car with the job?
physical or mental work?	working at the weekend?

Using these ideas and the contrasting sentences, describe and contrast these two jobs. Explain which you would prefer and why:
a doctor
b airline pilot

H Writing Tasks

1 You need to write an advertisement for a bicycle, which will explain why it is better than others – contrast it with Model X and Model Y, and explain why everybody would prefer to have your bicycle. It is called the Manta. (100-150 words)

2 You are looking for a job, and you have gone to a job agency, who want to help you. They have asked you to describe what sort of job you would most like to do, and what sort you would not. Contrast them in a short report. (100-120 words)

3 You want to go to Britain for the summer. The school you wrote to for information has two centres – one in the mountains of Scotland, and one by the sea in Cornwall. Write a letter saying which one you would prefer to go to and why. (100-120 words)

4 Look at the two advertisements opposite for summer holiday accommodation. Write a description, comparing and contrasting them, and discuss (120-150 words):
   a which you would prefer
   b which your family would prefer

Holidays in the SUN

Apartments Oro Negro
Playa de las Americas

Departures from Gatwick and Manchester

Location This modern apartment block opened in 1978 stands on the outskirts of Playa de las Americas. Walking into the town takes about 15 minutes, and to the beach 10 minutes.
Amenities Three bars. Plenty of lounge space with a cafeteria and excellent restaurant. Outside there are sun terraces and a large freshwater swimming pool.
Entertainment Dancing to live music several times a week.
Category Three-star.
Bedrooms Lift service to the apartments which are fully equipped for self catering and have a daily maid service.

Apartments for 4 persons (basic price as shown in price panel) with twin bedroom, lounge/dining area (with convertible couches for 3rd and 4th person), kitchenette (with oven), bathroom and balcony.   Supplement (on basic price) for occupancy by 3 persons £7 per person per week. Studio apartments for 2 persons with lounge/dining area (with convertible couches), kitchenette (with oven), bathroom and balcony, supplement (on basic price) £9 per person per week. Supplement (on basic price) for occupancy by 1 person £40 per week.
Apartment and breakfast.   Supplement for half board £25 per person per week.

Hotel Park Troya
Playa de las Americas

Departures from Gatwick and Manchester

Location Conveniently opposite a small beach at Playa de las Americas. Los Cristianos is just 3 miles up the coast and can be reached by regular local bus.
Amenities The air conditioned public rooms are smartly furnished and include spacious comfortable lounges, a long bar, and a restaurant serving an international menu. Outside you can relax on the sun terraces around the superb fresh water swimming pool or if you wish, stroll to the beach where there are sun umbrellas and chairs available for a small hire charge.
Entertainment There is occasional dancing to a live band in the hotel. The hotel has two tennis courts and there are facilities for water sports.
Children's facilities Children have their own playground and a shallow section of the pool. Early evening meals and baby sitting can be arranged.
Category Four-star.
Bedrooms Lifts serve all the floors and the well furnished bedrooms all of which have bathroom, balcony, piped music and telephone.

Twin bedded rooms with private bath, wc and balcony.   Single rooms with bath, wc and balcony, supplement £1.40 per night.
Half board.   Supplement for full board £1.20 per person per night.

9 Instructions
A Text

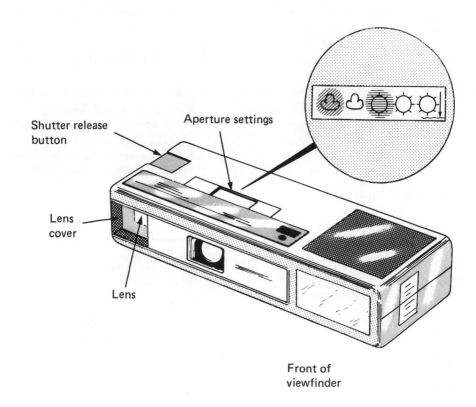

Shutter release button

Aperture settings

Lens cover

Lens

Front of viewfinder

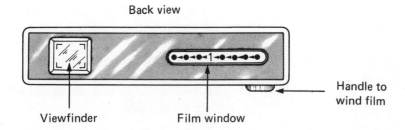

Back view

Viewfinder

Film window

Handle to wind film

In order to take photographs with your new Fotomatic 5, you must follow these simple instructions. First, take the film cassette out of its packet, and insert it into the back of the camera. Wind the film on until a number 1 appears in the film window at the back of the camera.

Now set the aperture to one of the five positions, marked by the sun or cloud signs, according to the lighting conditions. (Don't forget to take off the lens cover!)

Look through the viewfinder and move the camera until what you want to photograph appears between the white lines. Hold the camera steady and press the shutter release button slowly. There – that's all you have to do to get perfect pictures!

B Vocabulary

cassette	=	plastic box containing film (or tape)
insert	=	put something into something else
wind the film	=	turn the handle that moves the film along
aperture	=	the hole that lets the light into the camera
lens	=	the glass in front of the aperture, that collects the light
steady	=	firm, not moving

C Comprehension

1 What must you do first?
2 Where does the light enter the camera?
3 What do you look through when you take a photo?
4 Why are there different aperture positions?
5 What is the film kept in?

D Analysis

What do you think these five symbols mean? They are used to show the different positions of the aperture:

E Inference

1 Why is it necessary to hold the camera steady? What would happen otherwise?
2 What is the importance of pressing the shutter release button *slowly*?

F Discussion

1 Why do people want to take photographs at all? Why do you take them?
2 Apart from holidays, in what situations do people take photographs?
3 Is it necessary to have a very expensive camera? What difference does it make to the final photograph?

G Language Practice

1 There are different ways of giving instructions. In the text, the simplest form is used:
  Take the film cassette out of its packet.

  Another way is like this:
  You've got to take the film cassette out of its packet.
  But this is quite informal, and when you are writing you use the form:
  YOU HAVE TO TAKE THE FILM CASSETTE OUT OF ITS PACKET.
  Now re-write these sentences in the same way:*
  a You've got to insert the film into the camera.
  b You've got to wind the film on to number 1.
  c You've got to set the aperture.
  d You've got to open the lens cover.
  e You've got to look at the subject through the viewfinder.

2 If the instructions need to be more impersonal, you use the form:
  THE FILM CASSETTE SHOULD BE TAKEN OUT OF ITS PACKET.
  Now change the sentences a–e above to make impersonal instructions like this one.*

H Writing Practice

1 Sequencing

Look at this diagram. It shows a machine that sells small books of stamps. The instructions for the machine are written below, but they are in the wrong order. Re-write them in the correct sequence.

Lift the flap
Pull the knob
Wait till it drops
Take out the book of stamps
Put in 10p
Push it in again

2 Sequencing words

Some words are used to introduce sentences and show the correct sequence:

First you put in 10p, and then you've got to wait until it drops. After it drops, pull the knob out, then push it back in again. Before you can take out the book of stamps, you've got to lift the flap.

Now look at the camera instructions again. Write a set of instructions for a friend, and use these words to introduce the sentences:

before, after, then

It starts:

First you've got to take the film cassette. . .

3 Impersonal instructions

This recipe for making hamburgers is very informal. You want to re-write it in an impersonal way for a cookery book:

'Well, hamburgers are really very simple. All you need is a pound of minced beef, which you mix with the other things – salt and pepper, paprika, a teaspoon of mustard, Oh, and an egg as well. You break the egg in a bowl, of course, and mix all the things together with a fork. When it's smooth and well-mixed, make round hamburgers from the mixture, and roll them in some flour. Then you need a frying pan and some oil. Fry the hamburgers on both sides for about 15 minutes, until they're really brown. When they're ready, get some soft bread rolls and cut them in half. Put the hamburgers inside them and eat them as soon as possible.'

Now re-write this friendly recipe. First make a list of the ingredients, all the things you need to use. Then make a list of the instructions, in the right order. The first one is done for you:

1 Take one egg and break into a bowl.
2 etc

I Writing Tasks

1 Write the ingredients for your favourite recipe and write the instructions as you do for the hamburgers. Imagine it is for a serious book.

2 You are expecting an important American businessman to arrive at the airport in your country. He will need to know how to use a public telephone, so he can call you. Write a list of instructions. You will need words like these:

dial (the disc with numbers 0-9)
receiver (the thing you hold)
engaged (when the person you call is already talking to someone)

3 Look at this diagram and read the text. Together they explain how you should use this radio-cassette recorder. The instructions are very impersonal. Imagine your friend is going to borrow the recorder from you for the weekend, and you want to write a note explaining:

a how to use the radio.

b how to make a recording with the microphone.

Make the instructions less impersonal by using *You've got to. . .*, and show the right order by using *First, Then* etc.

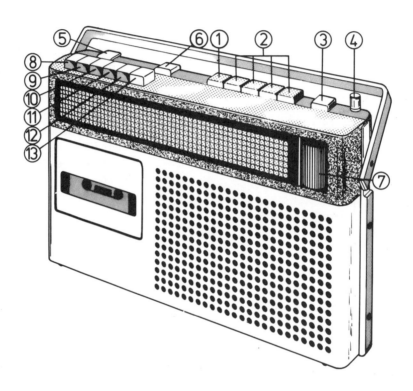

Radio Recorder

This radio recorder can receive radio programmes, record blank cassettes, and play back recorded cassettes.

Using the radio: switch the set on using one of the buttons marked 2 on the diagram. Select the waveband by pressing the button marked Long Wave, Medium Wave, Short Wave or FM. Turn the tuning control (7) to the radio station required. Pull out the aerial (4) for better reception.

Adjust the volume control (5) and the tone control (6) by sliding the controls to the left or right.
Switch off the radio with button (1).

Using the cassette recorder:
Press button (8) to open the compartment. Put in a cassette, and close the compartment. Press button (11) to playback a cassette. Press buttons (10) and (12) to move the tape quickly in either direction. To record, press the microphone (3) so it faces you. Press buttons (11) and (13) together and speak into the microphone. Do not speak too loudly, or the recording will be unclear. At the end of the recording, stop the tape with button (9).

10 Future plans

A Text

> VOTE FOR US!   VOTE FOR US!
>
> VOTE FOR THE PEOPLE'S PARTY!
>
> The People's Party is the only one that is interested in helping everybody – not just small groups of its friends. We have great plans for the future of this country, and this is what we will do if you elect us:
> * first we will reduce taxes – especially for the low-paid
> * we will improve the hospital service
> * we will build more houses, and help people to buy their own house
> * we will keep prices as low as possible
> * we will increase pensions in line with prices
> * we will make the cities safe at night, by improving the police force
> * we will stop the building of nuclear power stations
> * we will plan for a safe future – we will find alternative forms of energy
> * we will stop the use of animals in scientific experiments
>
> **Together we are going to make this a great country again, so vote for us!**

B Vocabulary

vote	= choose between different political parties and give your choice at the same time as everybody else, in an election
elect	= choose a person or party to represent you in the Parliament
pensions	= money paid by the State to old people
in line with	= in the same proportion as
nuclear power	= the power got from atoms of uranium
alternative	= other

C Comprehension

1 What is different about the People's Party – according to them?
2 How will they make life safer for everybody?
3 How will they make pensions worth more?
4 Who will gain most from the lower taxes?

D Analysis

1 What groups of people are the People's Party trying to attract most?
2 What is the criticism of nuclear power suggested by the text?

E Inference

They give no reason for wanting to stop the use of animals in scientific experiments – what reasons might there be?

F Discussion

1 This list of promises is called a manifesto. Do you think political parties want people to believe all these promises? Does the Party believe it can do all these things?
2 Do you think the People's Party could fulfill all these promises? Can you see any contradictions in their manifesto?

G Language Practice

1 Intentions

There are different ways of expressing your plans or intentions, depending on how definite you think they are:

Definite intention – I'm going to be rich

Not quite so definite – I'm planning to go away next week

Less definite – I'm hoping to visit Scotland/ I hope to visit Scotland

Now re-write the People's Party manifesto, using these sentences. Make three of each type.*

2 Forecasting

When talking about future events, you can't know what will happen, so you make a forecast – what you think will happen:

I'm sure it's going to rain tomorrow (*definite*)
I expect it'll rain tomorrow (*probable*)
I imagine it'll rain tomorrow (*less probable*)
I suppose it could rain tomorrow (*possible*)

Now use these sentences to write what you think about the People's Party manifesto. Use all of them to show what you believe they will or will not do.*

TELEVISION

BBC 1

2.00 FILM: A Challenge For Robin Hood
★ (1967), starring Barrie Ingham and James Hayter. Robin and his men fight a hated cousin.
3.35 The Gay Parisian: Ballet. **3.53 Regional News. 3.55 Play School. 4.20 Yogi Bear. 4.25 Jackanory. 4.40 The Bells Of Astercote. 5.35 Paddington. 5.40 News. 5.55 Nationwide.** (Regions vary until 6.20.)
6.50 Angels. 7.15 Terry And June Christmas Show. 7.45 Christmas Comedy Classic: The Likely Lads. (See facing page.)
8.30 The Dawson Watch. Les Dawson takes a look at Christmas. **9.00 News.**
9.25 Play For Today: Jessie. A story by Bryan Forbes, set in 1905, about the bond between a boy, dumb since birth, and a new maid who joins the family household. Starring Nanette Newman. (See facing page.)
10.55 Best Of British. Victorian and Edwardian ballads from Benjamin Luxon and Robert Tear. **11.35-11.40 News and Weather.**
BBC CYMRU/WALES: 4.45 Y Pibydd Brith. 5.00-5.40 Billboncyrs. 6.50 Heddiw. 7.10 Pobol Y Cwm. 7.40 Angels (as BBC 1 yesterday). 8.05 Angels (as today). 8.30-9.00 Terry And June. SCOTLAND: 8.30-9.00 Beechgrove Garden. 10.55-11.25 A Taste Of . . . Scotch And Wry.

BBC 2

6.35 One Hundred Great Paintings.
6.45 News.
6.55 Napoli. The romantic ballet performed by The Scottish Ballet.
8.45 Country Holiday. A sing-along of country music from the Snape Maltings, Suffolk.
9.25 Ireland: A Television History. Part 5: Famine.

H Writing Practice

1 Planning

When planning your time you need phrases like:
I can do that *from* 10.30 *to* 13.00.
I must finish that *by* Friday.
It doesn't start *until* 4 pm.

Look at this list of TV programmes for one evening. You want to plan your time so you can do three hours' work *and* watch as many programmes as possible between 5.30 and 12.00 in the evening. Use the phrases above to work out a plan for yourself, and choose the programmes you think are interesting.

Do it like this:
5.40 – I can watch the news, and then work for 1hr 5mins, until
7.00 – when I can watch . . .

LONDON

3.30 Look Who's Talking. 4.00 Get It Together. 4.45 Auditions (not colour).
5.45 News. 6.00 Thames News. 6.35 Crossroads.
7.00 World's Strongest Man. Ten heavyweight toughies compete for the title in New Jersey, America, with Geoff Capes muscling in for Britain. (See facing page.)
8.00 The Jim Davidson Show. Joker Jim with Tim Barrett, Hugh Paddick and Bob Todd. (See facing page.)
8.30 You're Only Young Twice. It's Christmas Eve in Paradise Lodge and Cissie Lupin (Pat Coombs) gets to play Father Christmas. Starring Peggy Mount.
9.00 Elvis—He Touched Their Lives. David Frost joins 350 members of the British Elvis Presley Fan Club on their annual pilgrimage to Memphis, Tennessee. **10.00 News.**
10.30 FILM: Farewell My Lovely (1975).
★ Starring Robert Mitchum as Raymond Chandler's tough detective Philip Marlowe, hired by an ex-convict to find his missing girlfriend. With Charlotte Rampling. (See facing page).
12.20-12.30 It's Christmas! Carols.

10.20 Christmas With The Fivepenny Piece. With special guest, folk-comedian Derek Brimstone.
10.50 News.
10.55-12.40 FILM: Pete 'n' Tillie (1972), starring
★ Walter Matthau in a witty comedy-drama about a wise-cracking advertising executive and his reluctant girlfriend (Carol Burnett).

2 Arranging a meeting

When you are arranging a meeting, you need the same phrases whether you are talking or writing to the other person:

Can you meet me on Friday at 10? (*formal*)
How about 4 on Thursday? (*less formal*)
Are you free Monday evening? (*less formal*)

Here are some replies to these questions:

I'm afraid I'm busy then. (*formal*)
I can't make it until after 7pm. (*less formal*)
I'm not free until 1pm. (*less formal*)
Yes, that would be fine.

Now use these phrases to complete this telephone conversation with a friend who is trying to arrange a meeting with you. The only times that you are free are Tuesday afternoon, Wednesday evening, Friday morning.

Jim:	Hello Robert, how are you? We must meet this week to talk about that conference. How about Monday or Tuesday mornings?
Robert:	. . .
Jim:	Well, the only other time I could make it would be Friday morning.
Robert:	. . .
Jim:	No, I couldn't make it before 10.30.
Robert:	. . .

I Writing Tasks

1 A friend is coming to visit you for a few days. Look at these advertisements from the local paper, and write a letter to her explaining what you both could do, what you would prefer, and asking what she would like to do. (80-100 words)

2 You are in business, and have just received this
letter:

Tuesday 24th April

Dear Alan,

It's very important that we meet as soon as
possible to discuss our new advertising
contract. I can get over to see you tomorrow,
Friday or Monday afternoon. Failing that, we
could perhaps meet at the weekend? Let me
know as soon as possible.

Yours,

Stuart

Here is your diary — now answer the letter.
(80-100 words)

SUN 22nd	Skiing 29th SUN
MON 23rd	15·00 Dentist 30th MON
TU 24th	1st TU
WED 25th Conference	Board Meeting 9·00 2nd WED
THU 26th	3rd THU
FRI 27th Visit Bristol office	4th FRI
SAT 28th Skiing	5th SAT

3 You are going to visit your uncle and aunt in Florida, USA for four weeks in the summer. You hope also to visit your sister and other American friends in different places. To get a visa, you must fill in this form, and outline your plans for the holiday – look at the notes at the bottom of the form. Write it out as a letter to the Embassy. (100-120 words)

THIS APPLICATION FORM IS SUPPLIED GRATIS

VISA APPLICATION

APPLICANTS SHOULD PRINT THE FOLLOWING INFORMATION

1. SURNAME   GIVEN NAME   MIDDLE NAME

2. OTHER NAMES *(Insert Maiden Name, Professional, Stage, Religious Name and Aliases)*

3. DATE OF BIRTH

MONTH	DAY	YEAR

4. RESIDENTIAL ADDRESS *(Include apartment no. and post zone)*

5. PLACE OF BIRTH *(City, State, (Country)*

6. NAME AND ADDRESS OF EMPLOYER OR SCHOOL

7. PASSPORT INFORMATION

PASSPORT NO._____

8. TELEPHONE AT RESIDENCE

9. OFFICE TELEPHONE

DATE ISSUED _____

10. SEX
☐ Female
☐ Male

11. COLOUR OF HAIR

12. HEIGHT

DATE EXPIRES _____

WHERE ISSUED _____

13. COMPLEXION *(fair, ruddy, olive, etc.)*

14. COLOUR OF EYES

15. MARKS OF IDENTIFICATION *(Visible Scars, Moles)*

16. NATIONALITY

17 MARITAL STATUS
Married ☐   Single ☐
Separated ☐   Widowed ☐   Divorced ☐

18. PRESENT PROFESSION OR OCCUPATION *(If Retired, State Past Profession)*

19. HAVE YOU EVER APPLIED FOR A UNITED STATES VISA OF ANY KIND? ☐ Yes ☐ No
(If YES state where and type of visa)

20. HOW LONG HAVE YOU LIVED IN THE U.K.?
_____Years _____Months

21. INDICATE WHETHER: Visa was granted ☐ or refused ☐
Application was abandoned ☐   Visa issued but subsequently cancelled ☐

22. WHEN DO YOU INTEND TO ARRIVE IN THE U.S.A.

23. NAME, RELATIONSHIP AND ADDRESS OF SPONSOR, FIRM, OR SCHOOL IN U.S.A.

24. WHAT IS THE PURPOSE OF YOUR TRIP?

25. WHO WILL PAY FOR YOUR TICKETS TO LEAVE THE U.S.A. at the end of your temporary visit? If not yourself, please explain.

26. HOW LONG DO YOU PLAN TO STAY IN THE U.S.A.?

27. HAVE YOU EVER BEEN THE BENEFICIARY OF AN IMMIGRANT VISA PETITION OR INDICATED TO A U.S. CONSULAR OFFICER A DESIRE TO IMMIGRATE TO THE U.S.A.?
If YES, please explain in an attached note.
Yes ☐ No ☐

28. HAVE YOU EVER BEEN IN THE U.S.A.?

☐ Yes ☐ No If YES, when, and for how long?

29. DO YOU INTEND TO WORK IN THE U.S.A.?

Yes ☐ No ☐
If YES, please give details

30. ARE ANY OF THE FOLLOWING IN THE U.S.A.? (If YES, what is their status: i.e., student, working, etc.)

☐ HUSBAND/WIFE_____   ☐ FIANCÉ/FIANCÉE_____   ☐ BROTHER/SISTER_____
☐ FATHER/MOTHER_____   ☐ SON/DAUGHTER_____

31. PLEASE LIST THE COUNTRIES WHERE YOU HAVE LIVED FOR MORE THAN ONE YEAR DURING THE PAST FIVE YEARS.

COUNTRIES   CITIES   APPROXIMATE DATES

32. TO WHAT ADDRESS DO YOU WISH YOUR VISA AND PASSPORT SENT?

VISITORS VISA INFORMATION

A VISA is necessary to apply for entry into the United States. Under U.S. law, all aliens seeking admission are presumed to require an immigrant visa unless they establish that they are entitled to receive a visa in one of the nonimmigrant categories. The most widely known nonimmigrant category is the VISITOR VISA, which is used by aliens who wish to enter the United States temporarily for business purposes or for tourism, visits to relatives and friends or similar reasons of pleasure. Other categories of nonimmigrant visas are required for persons with different temporary purposes of entry, such as students, participants in exchange programs, performing artists, professional journalists, representatives of foreign governments, etc.

TO APPLY FOR A VISITOR VISA

1   Complete this application form by PRINTING all of the answers. **(A SEPARATE APPLICATION IS REQUIRED FOR EACH TRAVELLER REGARDLESS OF AGE INCLUDING BABIES).**

2.   Submit your passport with the completed application form. Your passport should be valid for at least six months longer than your intended period of stay in the United States. A BRITISH VISITOR'S passport is **NOT** acceptable for American visa purposes since it is **NOT** valid for travel to the U.S.A.

3.   **PHOTOGRAPH.** A recent photograph 1½ inches square with your usual signature written on the REVERSE side must be affixed to the application form in the space provided. Children under the age of sixteen are not required to submit a photograph.

4.   Submit evidence substantiating the purpose of your trip and your intention to depart from the United States after a temporary visit. Examples of such evidence are (in cases of business trips) a letter from your employer or (in cases of pleasure trips) a letter from your employer verifying leave; a statement outlining your plans while in the United States and explaining the reasons why you would return abroad after a short stay, such as family ties, employment or similar binding obligations in your home country. U.S. law prohibits aliens who are granted visitor visas from working in the United States; they must, therefore, demonstrate that they have adequate funds of their own or assurances that they will be supported there by some interested person. In this connection, evidence should also be submitted regarding the arrangements you have made to cover your expenses while in the United States.

VISAS BY MAIL: You are urged, whenever possible, to apply for a VISITOR VISA without making a personal appearance at a Consular Office. Personal appearance may involve you in queuing and does not of itself ensure priority treatment. Complete this form after having carefully read all of the information contained there. Sign and date the form and *detach it from the information sheet*. Enclose all of the documentation requested above.

SUPPLY A SELF-ADDRESSED ENVELOPE — LARGE ENOUGH TO RETURN YOUR PASSPORT TO YOU. AFFIX SUFFICIENT POSTAGE TO THE ENVELOPE TO EXPEDITE THE RETURN OF YOUR PASSPORT.

NOTE If you are eligible, a VISITOR VISA will be stamped in your passport which will be returned to you promptly. If there is a question concerning your documentation or eligibility, you will be invited by mail or telephone to visit the Consular Office for a discussion of your plans to visit the USA for a temporary period.

**APPLY FOR YOUR VISITOR VISA EARLY AND BEFORE YOU MAKE FINAL TRAVEL ARRANGEMENTS.
ALLOW AT LEAST TWO WEEKS FROM THE DATE YOU MAIL YOUR PASSPORT AND APPLICATION
BEFORE MAKING ANY INQUIRIES.**

IN CASE OF EMERGENCY: When making a personal appearance for a VISITOR VISA for emergency travel to the United States, you must also submit documentary evidence to substantiate the need for such emergency travel.

Neither a vaccination against smallpox nor any other immunization is required for entry into the United States.

11 Formal letters

A Text

B Vocabulary

executive	=	a person who organises and makes decisions
scope	=	opportunity; chance to show how good you are
pay scales	=	lists which show who gets more or less pay because of age, experience etc
considerable	=	quite large
posts	=	jobs
GCE	=	General Certificate of Education – the English state exams, taken at 16 ('O' level) and 18 ('A' level)
at one sitting	=	exams taken at the same time (in the same year)
Civil Service	=	the British state administration

C Comprehension

1 What sort of job is offered in this advertisement?
2 What must you do before you can be interviewed?
3 Where will people taking these jobs probably work?
4 How can you earn extra money in this job?
5 Why is this job more interesting than it was before?

D Analysis

1 It is not clear *what* job is advertised. What do you think it could be? What would you do every day?
2 What sort of people do you think are wanted for the Civil Service?

E Inference

The advertisement mentions *promotion*, which will bring a lot of money. How do you think people can get this promotion? What would you have to do?

F Discussion

1 Would you like to do this sort of job? Why?
2 People who work for the Civil Service usually stay with their employers all their lives. Why do people do this, rather than change jobs every year?

G Language Practice

1 Formal vocabulary

Some words are more formal than others, and so are more often used in formal letters and writing:

Informal	Formal
job	post
get	obtain
large	considerable
want (= to expect)	require
want (= to desire)	wish

Now re-write this text, using the formal words instead of the informal ones:*
This job offers a large salary, and gives a good opportunity to someone who wants to get good experience. We want people who are enthusiastic and hard-working. Selling experience is preferred.

2 Introducing sentences

When two sentences are joined together, you can make the first one more interesting in this way:
I have seen your advertisement, and I would like to apply for the job.
HAVING SEEN YOUR ADVERTISEMENT, I WOULD LIKE TO APPLY FOR THE JOB.
I work in a bank, and I understand business.
WORKING IN A BANK, I UNDERSTAND BUSINESS.

You can only do this when the second sentence describes something caused by what happened in the first sentence. Now change these sentences in the same way:*
a I have learned Spanish, and I want to visit South America.
b He failed his exams, and he went back to school.
c She took the Civil Service test, and had an interview.
d He teaches in a school, and he knows a lot about children.

H Writing Practice

1 Beginning and ending a formal letter

Formal letters usually look a little different from informal letters (see Unit 1). Two things are usually added – the address of the person you're writing to, and your own name under the signature. Look at this example – Jack Barratt is writing to the manager of a hotel:

```
                                    24 Penrith Ave.,
                                    Chilforth

                                    November 5th

The Manager,
George Hotel,
High St.,
London.

Dear Sir,
. . . . . . .
. . . . . . .
                        Yours faithfully,
                            Jack Barratt
```

Look at the greeting in the letter – *Dear Sir*. You always use *Dear Sir* or *Dear Madam* if the person has a title like *The Manager*. You also use it if you know the name, but you don't know the person – you've not met them. And in this case you end the letter with *Yours faithfully*.

If you know the person, you start with:
Dear Mr Smith
Dear Mrs Smith (if she is married)
Dear Miss Smith (if she is not married)
Dear Ms Smith – many women like to be called *Ms*.
It is neutral, and doesn't show if she is married or not.
You end these letters with *Yours sincerely*.

Now practise beginning and ending these letters – remember it's different if you *know* the person:

a The manager /Barclays Bank/High St/Loxford – you don't know him

b Ms Baker, The Electricity Board/ Day St/Loxford – you know her

c Brian Davies/ Headmaster/Collins School/Loxford –you don't know him

d Alan Barker/ Planning Dept/ Town Hall/Loxford – you know him

e The Editor/Loxford News/High St/Loxford – you don't know him

2 Making requests

Often when you write a formal letter, you want someone to do something for you. You must make this request in a formal way. Here are some examples:

I'd be very grateful if you could. . .
I wonder if you could possibly. . .
I'd be obliged if you would. . .
Do you think you could. . .?

Now use these phrases, and the letter beginnings and endings, to write short letters:

a to ask the Tourist Office of Barbados to send you a travel brochure about the island.

b to ask the Cambridge Examination Board to send you some old exam papers. You are sending a cheque for £1. Write 'I enclose a cheque. . .'

I Writing Tasks

1 Look at these advertisements for jobs. Write a letter to apply for jobs. Each letter will be different – one of them is not very formal, so write an informal letter if you think it is better. (100-120 words)

BLUE BOAR HOTEL
Maldon

The Hotel is now under new management and we require the following staff.

SILVER SERVICE WAITER/WAITRESS

We require full time and part time staff. Some experience is essential and the positions are live out.

SECOND CHEF

The successful applicant will be responsible for the daily running of the kitchen in Head Chef's absence. The position is live in or out.

CHAMBER PERSON

We require a person to work full time in our Housekeeping department. This will include some weekend work, and the position is live out.

Would all applicants in the first instance apply by telephone to:
Mr or Mrs Robinson, Managers
BLUE BOAR HOTEL
Maldon 52681

SCOTAIR

STEWARDS/STEWARDESSES

We urgently need several of the above.

Requirements:

*Minimum age 21

*Maximum age 28

*Height between 5'3" and 5'11"

*One European language

*Good Education

*Smart appearance essential

If you are interested, 'phone Scotair Recruitment on 99-26734 between 9 and 5 on October 10th and 11th only.

2 Here is an advertisement for a degree course. Write a letter to the Registrar, explaining which subject(s) you would like to study, and why, and what you would do after the course. Make it very formal. (100-120 words)

3 Write a letter to your bank manager, explaining why you have no money in your account. Ask him to lend you money for a special reason, and justify your request. (100-150 words)

4 Look at this advertisement for a leather chair. You would like to buy it, but you want more information. You want to know how big it is, what sort of wood it is, what colour the leather is, and how long it would take to deliver. Write a letter asking these questions, and any other information you think you need. (80-100 words)

12 Reporting

A Text

These are the notes made by a policeman at the scene of a road accident. Read them carefully and then answer the questions. Some of the words are explained at the bottom of the page.

14.08   Emergency call - accident on A47 between Dunmow/Wallfield -
         2 cars and 1 lorry involved
14.09   Requested ambulance and fire engine
14.10   Left police station in car, with PC57
14.17   Arrived at scene of accident
         Ambulance and fire engine already arrived

<u>Situation</u>:   collision between lorry going north, car following,
           and car coming south

<u>Casualties</u>:   1 person killed (in green Ford)
           2 people injured (in blue Morris) - 1 trapped in car
           1 lorry driver shocked and slightly injured

<u>Road conditions</u>:   wet and slippery

<u>Cause</u>:   front left tyre of lorry had a puncture - lorry skidded
        across the road

14.19   Second ambulance arrived - first one left with injured and
         dead person

<u>Action</u>:   directed traffic
        radioed for photographer and crane
        PC57 spoke to people involved - see Interview Form
        PC57 filled in Accident Report Form

14.26   Trapped person freed - left in second ambulance
14.30   PC57 completed chalkmarks on road
         Police photographer arrived
14.45   Crane arrived to clear road
15.00   Road clear - returned to station

B Vocabulary

emergency   = serious or dangerous situation
collision   = crash, violent coming-together
casualities   = people killed or injured
slightly   = a little, not much (adverb)
slippery   = smooth, difficult to stand or
             move on
crane   = machine with a long arm for lift-
             ing heavy weights
skid   = slipping movement of the wheels
             of a car

C Comprehension

1 Where did the accident happen?
2 How many people were injured?
3 In which car was one person killed?
4 What were the road conditions like?
5 What direction was the lorry travelling in?
6 What was the cause of the accident?

D Analysis

Look at this drawing of the road accident, and then answer the questions.

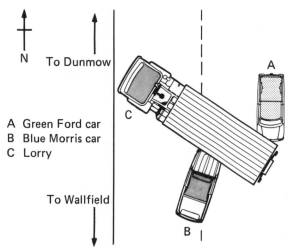

A Green Ford car
B Blue Morris car
C Lorry

1 Which vehicle caused the accident?
2 Which car probably hit the lorry first?
3 Why couldn't the blue car stop in time?
4 Why is the blue car on the right-hand side of the road?
5 Why was the green car more seriously damaged?

E Inference

Some information is not given in the text. But from the situation, and the information that *is* given, you can work it out. If you are not sure, explain what *probably* happened.

1 How many people went to hospital in the first ambulance?
2 Who freed the trapped person from the blue car?
3 Why did the policeman make chalk-marks on the road?

F Discussion

1 What could have prevented the accident?
2 How should the drivers have reacted to the road conditions?
3 What should the driver of the green car have tried to do?
4 Should lorries be banned from narrow roads like the A47?

G Language Practice

Look at this example:
   He was driving fast.
   HE SHOULDN'T HAVE BEEN DRIVING FAST.
Now change these sentences in the same way:*
a He was following the lorry very closely.
b He was looking out of the side window.
c He was driving without a seat-belt.
d The brakes were making a strange noise.

Look at this example:
   He wasn't wearing a seat-belt.
   HE SHOULD HAVE BEEN WEARING A SEAT-BELT.
Now change these sentences in the same way:*
a The windscreen wipers were not working properly.
b He wasn't concentrating on the road.
c The lorry wasn't using good tyres.
d He wasn't driving under 40mph.

H Writing Practice

1 Sequencing

Read these sentences. They describe what happened on the A47. But the sentences are not in the correct order. Re-write them in the order that they happened.
a The driver was killed instantly.
b It had a puncture.
c The road was blocked for an hour.
d A Morris travelling north also hit the lorry.
e It skidded across the road.
f The lorry was driving north.
g A green Ford travelling south hit the lorry.

2 Linking

Look at this example:

> The policeman directed the traffic. The ambulanceman helped the injured.
> THE POLICEMAN DIRECTED THE TRAFFIC WHILE THE AMBULANCEMAN WAS HELPING THE INJURED.

Now join these sentences in the same way:

a The photographer took pictures.
  The policeman made chalk-marks on the road.
b PC57 spoke to Mrs Smith.
  The firemen freed Mr Smith from his car.
c The second ambulance arrived.
  The first ambulance left.
d The policeman wrote his report.
  The crane cleared the road.

3 Reporting what people say

When you write down what someone has said to you, you must change the form of the sentence. Look at this example:

> John said, 'I crashed my car on Saturday'.
> JOHN SAID HE HAD CRASHED HIS CAR ON SATURDAY.

Now read what the two drivers, Mr Smith and Mr Goodman, said about the accident. Write down what they said, in the same way as in the example.

Mr Smith: 'I heard a loud bang and then saw the lorry skid across the road. I felt a pain in my knee – but I don't remember anything else.'

Mr Goodman: 'I heard a loud bang, and felt the lorry start to skid. I think the wheels stopped turning. I smashed my head on the windscreen. I don't know what happened after that.'

Policemen have to fill in Interview Forms after an accident, where they repeat what people have said to them. Make your own form and report what Mr Smith and Mr Goodman said.

```
INTERVIEW FORM

Name: _____

Time: _____

_____

_____
```

4 Writing reports

The policeman who was at the scene of the accident has to re-write his notes as a report, using full sentences, and writing in a formal, impersonal way. For example:

14.08   Emergency call – accident on A47 between Dunmow/Wallfield – 2 cars & 1 lorry involved.

In the report this will be:

'At 14.08 there was an emergency call. The caller said that there had been an accident on the A47 between Dunmow and Wallfield. There were two cars and one lorry involved in the accident.'

Now practise writing in this way, and finish the policeman's report (page 54) for him.

Write another formal report from the notes below. These were written by a newspaper reporter sitting in a courtroom, listening to a murder trial. Write a short report from these facts:

Don Sullivan, 35, killed wife/ found her with his best friend/ been having an affair for two years/ Sullivan lost control/hit her with hammer/ very unhappy in court/ judge sentenced him to ten years.

I Writing Tasks

1 Mrs Smith wrote a letter to her mother, describing what happened (see H3, this page). Here is the beginning and end of the letter – now write the rest of it (100-120 words):

> Dear Mum,
> Something terrible happened yesterday. . .
> . . .
> . . .
> Yours ever,
>   Doris

2 Imagine you are a fireman, returning from a serious fire in a supermarket. Write a report of what happened. (100-150 words)

3 Imagine you are a reporter for the local radio station. Write a report describing what happened when someone famous came to visit the town. Pick your own famous person – but make it a serious report. (100-150 words)

4 Imagine you have seen a UFO – a flying saucer from Space. Write a report of it for a magazine. It is a serious magazine, so write a serious report, so that people will believe you. (150-200 words)

13 Summarising

A Text

Father saves family as fire sweeps their home

By CHRIS PAYNE

A MAN led his two children and wife to safety as fire swept part of their Colchester home.

And in another blaze in the town, a couple were made homeless.

The first fire, early yesterday, happened as 33-year-old taxi driver Jim Eastwood and his wife Kay, 31, lay asleep in their home at Prince Philip Road, Monkwick.

Mrs Eastwood, who was first to wake, got up, felt heat coming from downstairs.

Mr Eastwood rushed downstairs to try to put out the blaze, which was sweeping through the kitchen of his council home, but the smoke and heat were too intense.

Mrs Eastwood got her children Maria, nine, and Russell, 12, from their bedrooms and they hung out of a window gasping for air.

"There was nothing else we could do by that time as the smoke was gagging us," said Mrs Eastwood.

AAB taxi driver, Mr Eastwood, who dialled 999 while downstairs, then decided to climb out of his bedroom window to lead his wife and children to safety.

"I got out of the window first and climbed onto a ledge above the downstairs living room. I then lifted and helped the children and my wife out," he added.

"I was ready to jump down into the garden, but our next door neighbours were awake by then and opened their bedroom window and let us in," he added.

In the other blaze this morning, fire badly damaged a back-room at Rose Villa in Artillery Street and destroyed records and furniture.

A fire brigade spokesman said the occupants of the house, Daniel and Kim Saunders, were made homeless.

B Vocabulary

fire swept	=	fire spread through
blaze	=	fire
council home	=	house owned by the State
gasping	=	breathing quickly with an open mouth
gagging	=	stopping us from breathing
ledge	=	a narrow shelf coming out from the wall
occupants	=	people living in the house

C Comprehension

1 When was the fire at Mr Eastwood's house?
2 Where did this fire start?
3 When was the other fire, and where did it start?
4 How did the Eastwood family escape?
5 What was the major problem of the other family?

D Analysis

1 What are the differences between the two fires? Make a list of the facts that are different – What are the important differences?
2 What effect did the *time* of the fire have in each situation?

E Inference

No information is given about the causes of the fires. What could be the cause in each case? What is suggested by the different situations?

F Discussion

1 The newspaper gives much more space to the fire in the Eastwood's house, although it is the other family who are homeless. Why do you think this is?
2 Why do you think newspapers put disasters like this on to the front page? Why are people interested in these things?
3 The newspaper also describes the ages and jobs of one family – why?

G Language Practice

1 Embedding

One way of joining sentences, and making them more interesting, is to put one inside the other:

A man was identified yesterday as John Brown. His body was found in the forest.
A MAN, WHOSE BODY WAS FOUND IN THE FOREST, WAS IDENTIFIED YESTERDAY AS JOHN BROWN.

Now join these sentences in the same way:*
a The woman sold her sports car today. Her husband was killed in a car crash.
b The town has given a special dinner for the footballers. The football team won the FA Cup.
c Sir Laurence Olivier has received an Oscar award. His acting is known all over the world.
d Roberto Leone died today. His paintings of the Queen made him famous.
e The pop group 'Cannon' have refused to appear on television. Their new record is at the top of the charts.

2 Headlines

Headlines are sometimes like notes – they are short versions of sentences, with some words missing. Look at the headline in the text. Can you work out which words are missing?

The headline should be:

A father saves his family as a fire sweeps their home

So the missing words are: *a* and *his*
Others are often missed out – *a, the, his, her, their, is, was, were, has, have, has been, have been.*

Now re-write these headlines as normal English:*
a Workers warned today about strike
b New taxes introduced by Government
c Ten people killed yesterday in car crash
d Woman lost dog in forest
e Theatre to close if no money found

H Writing Practice

1 Taking notes

The first step in summarising, whether it's a lecture or a story you want to summarise, is to take notes about the facts.
For example, the text about the fire contains much more than the necessary facts. So the first thing is to take notes about the necessary facts, facts that tell us about the fire:
– fire in Prince Philip Road
– Eastwood family asleep
– man saved wife and two children
Now make notes about the other facts in the same way.

2 Writing a summary

The next step is to make proper sentences from your notes, and join them together in some of the different ways you have learned in the course:

There was a fire in Prince Philip Road yesterday. Mr Eastwood saved his wife and two children by climbing out of the window.

Now give the rest of the details of the fire, by writing sentences from the notes you made in 1 above, and join them together.

3 Condensing

The summary you write might still be too long, so you need to find ways of making it shorter. One way is to take out adjectives:

Attractive mother of two Mrs Stella Jones became the *proud* owner of a *lovely new* dishwasher after winning an *exciting* competition at the opening of Tesco's *huge new* supermarket.

This report is 29 words long. Take out the adjectives, which are not very important, and it is only 24 words long.

Another way is to take out unecessary information, such as ages, physical description, and facts that don't add a lot to our understanding of what happened. Look at this example:

Mrs Eastwood got her children ~~Maria, nine, and Russell, twelve,~~ from their bedrooms and they hung out of the window ~~gasping for air.~~
~~There was nothing else we could do by that time,~~ the smoke was gagging us,' said Mrs Eastwood.

By taking out the words shown, the text is reduced from 41 words to 23 words.

Now practise this by shortening this story: it has 183 words. Reduce it to a maximum of 120 words.

I Writing Tasks

1 Write a summary of the main text about the fire. Write first a summary of the basic facts, maximum 50 words. Then write a description with a maximum of 100 words.

2 Imagine you work for the tourist office in your home town. You are asked to write an English history of your town – write it as a summary of about 150 words.

3 Write a summary of this newspaper story, in not more than 100-110 words. Add a headline to the story (not more than seven words).

Coggeshall head-on crash kills two

TWO men died when two cars collided head on, an inquest was told.

The double death happened on the A120 opposite the Queen's Head public house outside Coggeshall. Samuel Clay, 67, of Pole Barn Lane, Frinton, director of a cleaning firm, was a passenger in a car driving towards Braintree. He died immediately from multiple injuries.

The driver of the car, company director Mr Vernon St John, of Queen's Road, Frinton, was seriously injured

PNEUMONIA

The driver of the other car, Paul Barker, a 22-year-old demonstrator, of Great Missenden, Bucks, died in hospital a month after the accident. Consultant pathologist Dr John Stewart said Mr Barker died from bronchial pneumonia caused by injuries received in the crash.

Mr St John told the Colchester inquest that Mr Barker's car pulled out to overtake a van on a corner. " The car suddenly darted out from behind the wagon. I remember braking and trying to get on to the verge, but there wasn't an earthly chance of avoiding the collision," he said.

Coroner Dr Charles Clark recorded a verdict of accidental death.

BIRD fancier Ronald Royce's feathers were ruffled when he discovered twelve of his pet canaries were missing one day.

And three days later another bird keeper in the same village discovered 13 of his canaries missing as well.

The mystery was solved when police interviewed two youngsters who admitted stealing the birds from their aviaries.

They and some friends eventually returned the birds voluntarily to their owners, Mr Donald Oates, prosecuting, told Colchester Juvenile Court yesterday.

The boys, aged 13 and 14, and both from Tolleshunt Knights, admitted stealing 12 canaries, 20 feeders, a cage, a carrying box, a tin of seed, a magnet and three nest pans belonging to Ronald Royce of Tiptree.

COSTS

They also admitted stealing 13 canaries and three cages belonging to Peter Rowe and on another day stealing groceries from the Colchester Co-op.

They were each ordered to pay a total of £23 in fines compensation and prosecution costs.

The 14-year-old told the court he belonged to the Royal Society for the Protection of Birds and hoped to own some himself one day.

The 13-year-old said he took the birds " in a moment of impulse."

4 This description of the history of tea is about
500 words long. Prepare two summaries of it —
a the bare facts (40-50 words)
b a summary of 150 words

The Story of Tea

Almost everyone in the world drinks tea, from astronauts to aquanauts, from Chinese to Russians, Persians and Indonesians.

Workmen strike if they can't get it. Armies stop for it. Housewives 'live' on it. Grannies pour it with reverence.

People brew it in pots, urns and samovars. In the air, on mountain tops, amid the cities, out in the fields and in submarines in the depths of the oceans people pour boiling water on small mounds of dark coloured leaves to infuse the drink that has been popular for centuries.

They drink it 'neat', or with mint, lemon or jasmine. Some even pour rancid yak butter into it!

But the most famous nation of tea drinkers - the British - choose to mix it with milk and sugar.

Fittingly, it was two British housewives who set a world tea drinking record. They spent six testing hours in a television studio, downing a total of $6\frac{1}{2}$ gallons between them in their attempt. That was in 1970, and the winner gulped her way to the title by emptying an incredible 78 canteen-size 'cuppas'.

No-one knows when tea was first discovered, or how it came to be such a popular drink - the average Briton downs five cups a day - but it has its own folklore as well as an indelible place in the history books.

The beverage is generally accepted to have originated in China hundreds of years ago. Records going back to the fourth century A.D. refer to tea - for instance, a well-known general wrote to his nephew to complain that he was feeling old and depressed and wanted some real *t'u* to liven him up.

By the eighth century A.D. most Chinese were drinking tea, both because they liked it as a beverage and for its medicinal value. Tea was so popular that one of the most distinguished poets of the T'ang dynasty, a chap called Lu Yu, even wrote a Holy Scripture about it. It was called Ch'a Ching, which translated means Tea Scripture.

Over the years the habit of drinking tea spread around the world as explorers and travellers went to China and India and then returned to their own countries with some of the leaves.

The first cup of tea ever sampled in Britain was probably tasted in the elegant surroundings of a house which used to stand on the site now occupied by Buckingham Palace, the home of our Kings and Queens.

Gradually, as the world's trade routes developed and more supplies were imported, the price of tea went down and, by the middle of the 18th century, it had become the popular family drink. It ousted its great rival, coffee, which had arrived in Europe earlier and which had given rise to the famous 'coffee houses' in England.

The growing popularity of tea changed its 'social status'. Tea parties became all the rage. Tea and coffee houses opened where people could enjoy a 'cuppa' and a chat in much the same way that many now go to the local public house for a glass of beer.

14 Giving advice

A Text

The energy problem is a lot of hot air. True or false?

Don't waste heat in rooms that aren't being used. Check radiators are turned down.

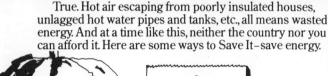

True. Hot air escaping from poorly insulated houses, unlagged hot water pipes and tanks, etc., all means wasted energy. And at a time like this, neither the country nor you can afford it. Here are some ways to Save It—save energy.

Switch off one bar on the fire. Your family won't notice, but your electricity bill will.

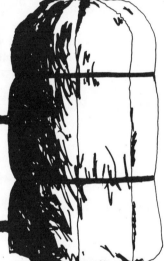

Nobody will be able to tell the difference if you turn down your heating a couple of degrees. Except you when the bills turn up!

Fit a 3-inch lagging jacket. An unlagged water tank can cost you about £1 a week in wasted energy.

Save It by insulating your roof. It's a dirty job up there in the attic. But since that's where 25% of heat escapes, it's well worth the trouble. Watch out for Barry Bucknell's tips on TV.

Draughts from windows can be a real pain in the neck. They mean wasted heat too. But don't block window or wall ventilators, and check that there is adequate ventilation before fitting draught excluders in any rooms with gas or other fuel burning appliances.

It can easily be curtains for a lot of the heat loss from windows. All you have to do is draw them.

At work too, make it your business to Save It wherever you can with safety. Look for waste in lighting, heating, and machinery left running when it's not needed.

There's another place you can Save It. In your wallet. Because the more energy you save for the country, the more money you save on your fuel bills. That's energy sense.

Energy sense is common sense.

Issued by the Department of Energy.

B Vocabulary

hot air	=	also means 'nonsense'
poorly	=	badly
insulated	=	protected from cold or heat
unlagged	=	unprotected (pipes), not insulated to keep heat in, or cold out
attic	=	the space of the roof of a house
draughts	=	air that comes round the edge of doors or windows
the bills turn up	=	the bills arrive

C Comprehension

1 Why should you close your curtains when it is evening?
2 What is the main advantage of stopping draughts in your house?
3 What is the advantage of insulating the roof of a house?
4 How do all these suggestions save energy? What sort of energy will be saved?
5 Does the writer of the advertisement think there is an energy problem or not?

D Analysis

1 Why should energy be saved? What advantages are there in this?
2 Which actions does the writer of the advertisement think are the most important in saving energy?

E Inference

There is no name at the bottom of the advertisement. Who do you think planned, wrote and paid for this, and why?

F Discussion

1 The energy problem is often discussed in newspapers etc. What are the different problems and solutions that have been described?
2 One of the problems connected with energy is that many people waste energy, by using cars when they needn't, by throwing away materials that could be used again. What can be done about this?

G Language Practice

1 Giving advice

Here are some examples of giving advice:
  If you want to pass your driving test,
  a *you'd better* have a lot of lessons
  b *you should* have a lot of lessons
  c *you ought to* have a lot of lessons

Make sentences in the same way from these words:*
a you/go to university/ pass examinations
b he /work in USA/work permit first
c you/ be successful/get up early
d they/make a lot of money/start their own business

Here are some more examples:
  If I were you I'd do this.
  I think you ought to do this.
  I'd advise you to do this.

Practise giving advice to someone who wants to be rich/more beautiful/famous/to live a long time.

2 Suggesting

If someone has a problem, your advice might include a suggested solution to the problem:

Problem	*Suggestion*
I don't feel well	1 You should go to the doctor
	2 Why don't you go to the doctor?
	3 You could go to the doctor

The numbers show a scale of advice/suggestion: 1 is a strong suggestion, the others are not so strong. 3 is a gentle suggestion, with the stress on *could*.

Imagine you are replying to a friend's letter, and write strong or weak suggestions to solve these problems:*
a I'm too fat and unfit.
b I never have enough money to pay my bills.
c My flat is always very cold.
d My car never starts in the morning.

H Writing Practice

1 Criticising

Before you can give advice, you often need to criticise what someone is doing wrong. You use sentences like:

Don't do that, it's dangerous.
You shouldn't do that, it's dangerous.
Avoid doing that, it could be dangerous.

Use these sentences to criticise and give advice on safety in the kitchen, to go with this picture. Use the list of Do's and Don't ideas.

Do's

Keep the kitchen clean.
Keep cleaning liquids away from children.
Put wall cupboards low enough to reach them.
Have a fire extinguisher ready.

Don'ts

Don't polish the floor.
Don't leave water on the floor.
Don't let children play with the cooker.
Don't leave hot fat in a pan when you go out.

2 Analysing

You can't give advice until you know what the problem is. So you must analyse the parts of the problem, perhaps make a list of them so you can answer them.

Look at this problem letter from a newspaper:

Dear Problem Page,

I'm so worried about my boyfriend that I can't sleep at night. I'm sure he doesn't really like me very much, because he still thinks about his first girl friend a lot. She left him about six months ago, and he's still in love with her. He gets unhappy if anyone mentions her name and I think he wants to go out with her again. I'm unhappy because he won't take me out in the evenings – he says he's saving money. And now he tells me he will never marry anyone but this girl. What should I do? I still like him a lot.

Julia

What are the different problems of the boy and the girl? Make two lists:

Boy's problems	Girl's problems
1 His first girlfriend left him	He won't marry her
2	
3	

Now write a letter to the girl, giving advice on each of these problems.

I Writing Tasks

1 Your friend has just passed his/her driving test, and is going to buy a car. Write a letter (100-120 words) giving advice about what things to be careful about when buying a car – things that can be dangerous. Here are some words you will need:
brakes tyres lights mirrors seat belts large windows windscreen washer rear window heater strong bumpers

2 You have just received this letter from somebody you know. Write a reply, pointing out the problems and giving advice (150-180 words):

I'm in a terrible mess. I've just lost my job because I had an argument with the boss. He wanted me to work at the weekend but I'd arranged to go to London for the weekend. I told him he was crazy to ask me to work on Saturday and he sacked me!

On top of that the car broke down on the way home from work – I forgot to put any water in the radiator. My girlfriend was very angry about it, and I called her an idiot who knew nothing about cars, she said she didn't want to see me ever again.

What on earth shall I do? I must get another job soon because I've got to pay the repair bills.

Yours,
Colin

P.S. My landlady says I've got to leave my flat at the end of the month, because I make too much noise with my record player. Isn't she stupid?

3 You have a friend in America who wants to come to your country to live and work. Write a letter giving advice on what he/she should do to get a job, and what he/she needs to know to live happily in your country (120-150 words).

4 You have been asked to write a short leaflet on road safety for young students who are going cycling in Britain. Give advice on what they should and should not do – write it in an informal way (120-150 words).

To help you, here are some of the rules for cyclists from the British Highway Code:

Extra rules for cyclists

130 Make sure your cycle is in good condition—particularly the brakes, tyres, lamps and rear reflector—before you ride it.

131 Do not start off, turn right or left, or pull up without first glancing behind to see it is safe. Give a clear signal of what you mean to do.

132 Do not ride more than two abreast. Ride in single file on busy or narrow roads.

133 On busy roads, if you want to turn right, it is often safer to pull well into the left side of the road and wait for a safe gap in the traffic in both directions before you start to cross.

134 While riding:

    (*a*) always hold the handlebar and keep your feet on the pedals;

    (*b*) do not hold on to another vehicle or another cyclist;

    (*c*) do not carry a passenger unless your cycle has been built or altered to carry one;

    (*d*) do not ride close behind another vehicle;

    (*e*) do not carry anything which may affect your balance;

    (*f*) do not lead an animal.

135 If there is an adequate cycle path beside the road, ride on it.

---

15 Persuading
A Text

The Gold Star Breakfast

There's nothing wrong with champagne at breakfast time. In fact, it's a very refreshing start to the day. Champagne is, however, a little more expensive these days. So it's a comforting thought for our passengers to know beautifully chilled French champagne is theirs for the asking, at any time of day or night.

It's all part of our Gold Star Service for businessmen on long-distance flights - and it costs no more than economy class travel. But with free champagne how can we call it economy class?

B Vocabulary

comforting = it makes you feel better
chilled = cooled quite a lot, but not frozen
theirs for the asking = free
economy = economy class is the cheapest way to fly

C Comprehension

1 What is this advertisement trying to sell?
2 What is Gold Star Service?
3 Why do the writers of the advertisement think it is wrong to call their normal service 'economy'?
4 Does Gold Star Service cost more?

D Analysis

1 The passenger in the advertisement is wearing pyjamas. What effect does this have? What do you think when you see it?
2 Why do you think the airline wants to show its passengers like this?
3 Apart from pyjamas, what else is casual or unusual about the picture of the passenger?

E Inference

Champagne is very expensive. Why do you think this airline wants to give it away free?

F Discussion

1 Free gifts, like free champagne, are often given away by people trying to sell things. What reasons are there for this?
2 If you were flying somewhere, would you prefer free champagne or a cheaper ticket?

G Language Practice

1 Suggesting

The first step in persuading someone to do or buy something is to make a suggestion:

Informal:

Why don't we go horse-riding?
How about going horse-riding?
Let's go horse-riding.

Formal:

You should buy Leyland cars!
Why not try Leyland cars?
We suggest you buy a Leyland car.

Now practise making suggestions from these words:*
a we/dinner/party/ (*informal*)
b you/camping/Wales (*informal*)
c you/try/Donaldson's soups (*informal*)
d we/meet/discuss business (*formal*)
e you/buy/Suno TV sets (*formal*)

2 Persuading

Here are some ways of persuading people to do things, or buy things:

You'll really enjoy seeing this film
You *must* see this film – it's very good
You really ought to see this film
Don't you think you should buy a new car?
Perhaps you ought to buy a new car?

Another way is to exaggerate the qualities of the thing you are describing, using words like:

amazing, fantastic, incredible, excellent, wonderful, terrific, unbelievable

Now practise persuading people, by making sentences about these things:*
a going camping
b going on a diet
c buying a new LP
d learning to play the piano
e buying a stereo cassette recorder

H Writing Practice

1 Emphasising quality

In order to persuade people, you often need to stress how good something is:

It's *really* good.
It's *very* reliable.
It's made of the *highest quality* materials.
Tennis is *excellent* exercise and *great* fun.

Use some of these words to persuade people to:
a go mountain-climbing
b buy your motorcycle

2 Advertisements

Advertisements are usually trying to persuade you to buy an object or a service. To do this they often:
- suggest the product will make you happy
- suggest the product will save you money
- claim it is the best product you can buy
- suggest something bad may happen if you don't buy it
- suggest you will be more popular if you buy it

Now look at this advertisement, and describe what it is trying to persuade you about:

Available at Boots, Department Stores and leading chemists.

3 Giving reasons

Here are some ways of explaining *why* one thing is better than another:

This car is better due to its reliability.

This bicycle is better *because it's got* five gears.

More people are travelling by train *because of* the price of petrol.

The reason for the price increase is higher wages.

Use these phrases to expand these notes on Canada. They explain why Canada is considered a very good place to live. Write a short text giving all the reasons:

Canada

below \ average divorce rate
above average number of cars per 100 people
high number of TVs per 100 people
lowest population density of industrial countries
high number of students at university
very low suicide rate

70

I Writing Tasks

1 Your cousin has written to you, explaining that he wants to leave his wife and family and live with someone else. Write to him to try and persuade him not to do it. Give a lot of reasons. (100-150 words)

2 Look at this advertisement, and then write a description (80-100 words), explaining:
   who it is persuading
   what it is persuading them to do/think
   how it is successful

3 You are working for an advertising company. They want you to write an advertisement for an electric shower, and they give you these facts. Write an advertisement that will persuade people to have showers and not baths. (80-100 words)

Facts: hot water in five seconds
        own water heater
        five litres per minute of water
        costs 2p for five minutes
        installed in one day
        wide range of shower curtains/doors

4 You have received a letter from your employer explaining that the company wants to save money, and so they are sacking fifty people. You are one of them. Write a reply, persuading them to change their mind (100-120 words). Give reasons.

Phillip gave her
everything
   a romantic dinner,
   a gold ankle bracelet,
   all his best lines,
   and his bad breath.
Sorry Phil.

He should have remembered
Double Amplex.
Available from Chemists throughout the U.K. and the Republic of Ireland.

16 Describing processes

A Text

Making a record

There are many different steps in the making of a record. Here is a description of the process that brings records into the shops:

1 The musicians play and sing. The sound they make is picked up by the microphones (about 16-20 of them).

2 The sounds are changed into electricity and sent through wires to the mixer, where they are made louder or quieter.

3 The signals are then sent to the tape recorder, which records them on to 16 tracks on the tape. All the instruments are kept separate.

4 Afterwards, the recordings are mixed again, and a new tape is made, with only two tracks (stereo). Some sounds are placed on the 'left' of the tape, so they can be heard from the left loudspeaker.

5 This stereo tape is taken to the cutting machine. This cuts a groove into a piece of metal. Two pieces of metal are cut – one for Side One and one for Side Two of the record.

6 This metal disc with grooves is then used to make another metal disc – with ridges.

7 From this metal disc (called a father) a steel disc with grooves is made. This is called a mother. It is played by the engineeers, and the sound quality is checked.

8 From the mother, two son discs are made, and are put into a pressing machine with some black plastic in the midde.

9 The press is heated, and the plastic melts and flows between the ridges of the metal discs. So a plastic record is made, with grooves cut into each of its sides. This is cooled with water and taken out.

10 The record is put into a sleeve and sent to the record shop.

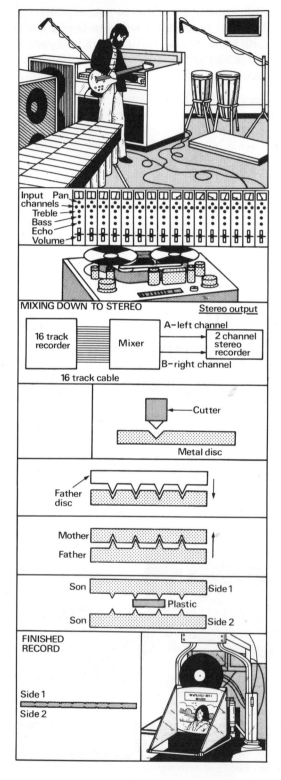

B Vocabulary

process = a way of doing things
track = part of the tape, like lines side by side
signal = sound which had been changed into electricity
groove = a cut, shaped like a triangle, that goes across something
disc = something round and thin
ridge = opposite of a groove; the raised part of something
melt = become liquid when it is hot
sleeve = where you put your arm in a coat; *here* the paper cover for a record

C Comprehension

1 What can change music into electricity?
2 What is the difference between the first and the second tape recording?
3 Why are two metal discs cut to make one record?
4 Why do engineers make a 'mother' disc?
5 How is the final record actually made?

D Analysis

1 Why do you think all the instruments and voices are kept separate on 16 tracks?
2 Why do you think a second tape is made, to reduce 16 tracks to 2?

E Discussion

1 Sometimes musicians listen to the first recording, and then add more instruments or more voices. Why do you think they do this? Couldn't they record everything at once, and use more people?
2 The mixer can place some sounds on the left and some on the right, so you hear different things from your two stereo loudspeakers. Do you think this is unnatural? Would you prefer to hear the music as it was played in the studio?

F Language Practice

1 Describing a process

A process is usually carried out by people, but it is described in an impersonal way:
  The sound *is picked* up by the microphone.
  The record *is pressed* by melting plastic.
If one step in the process is very important, it can be described like this:
  The mother disc *must be checked* for quality before the record is pressed.
Now describe the processes below, using sentences like those above:

Making bread

a wheat/plant/May (*important*)
b wheat/harvest/September
c it/transport/mill
d it/ground/flour (*important*)
e flour/take/bakery
f flour/other things/bake/bread

2 Sequencing

Sequencing words show the order in which things happen. Some were used in Unit 9 – look back at them. Here are some other ways of showing the order of actions:
  As soon as the tape is finished, it is taken to the cutting machine.
  After being checked, the mother disc is used to make son discs.
  Before being mixed together, the sounds are kept separate on 16 track tape.

Now use these sentences to join together the steps in this process:*
a the gas is turned on/the gas is lit.
b the pan is filled with water/is placed on the cooker.
c the water has boiled/the pan is taken off.
d the tea-leaves are put into the teapot/hot water is poured over the tea.
e the tea is left for two minutes/the tea is served.

G Writing Practice

1 Taking notes

Before you can describe all the steps in a process, you need to sort out all the necessary information. Often this means taking notes from a longer text with a lot of unnecessary information.

Read this text, and then make notes, in the form of a list of the most important steps in the process:

Paper-making

Modern paper is manufactured from a mixture of various fibres like rags, linen, wood, waste paper. The main ingredient is of course wood pulp, produced from complete trees after the bark has been removed. The main areas of production are Finland and Canada, where the trees are cut down, taken to the saw mill, and chopped up. The pieces of wood are then ground up and mixed with water to make wood pulp. This is mixed with other substances, such as glue, to make a paper fibre mixture, and then poured out on to wire screens. These are large areas of wire mesh — sheets of metal with a large number of holes in them. Here the water is extracted from the mixture, which is dried and passed through many rollers to press it into shape. This process produces one continuous sheet of paper, which is wound into a large roll at the end of the manufacturing process.

2 Sequencing

It is important to get the steps of a process in the right order, using the words practised above. These steps are out of order – write them again in the right order and add the sequence words:

Cotton

a clothes are made from the finished cotton.
b the seeds are removed.
c the cotton is spun into thread.
d cotton is picked from the bushes.
e the thread is woven into cloth.
f it is transported to the mill, to be spun.

3 Describing diagrams

Many processes are described by diagrams, with the steps underneath the pictures. Add the describing sentences to this diagram, using the language learned above:

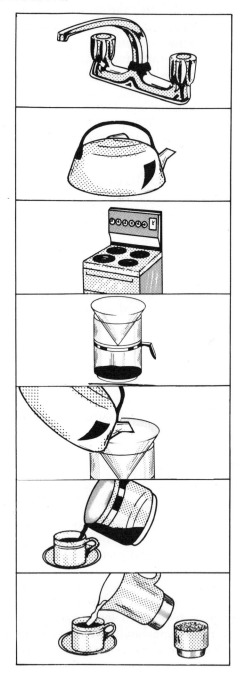

H Writing Tasks

1 The diagram below shows how sounds and actions are transmitted and shown on your television. Write a description to go with the picture. (120-150 words)

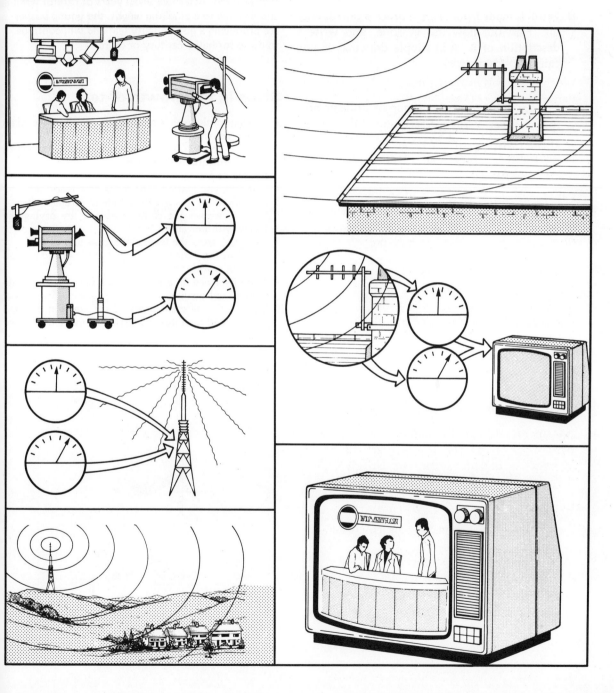

2 You are lending your stereo system to a friend while you are on holiday. To make sure that he understands what it does, you write out a description of how it works – the process that leads to sounds coming from the loudspeaker. Don't write instructions – write an impersonal process. (100-120 words)

3 Petrol is made from oil by a process called refining. Find out how this is done, and write a description of it. Add simple drawings if you can. (120-150 words)

4 You are going to teach a group of students how to drive a car. Write a description of the process you must go through to start a car, drive it, use the gears and brakes etc. Keep it impersonal. (120-150 words)

5 Look at the pictures opposite of how tea is produced. Use the pictures opposite and the words below to write a text describing the process. (120-150 words)

Tea comes from the evergreen plant Camellia Sinensis. The cuttings are carefully nursed for about 18 months, then planted. After five-seven years of careful tending and pruning to a plucking height, the young bushes are producing a good quality leaf and will continue to do so for half a century or more.

Steps in the growth of tea

1 **Picking** – only fresh leaves are picked. These are taken to the factory.
2 **Drying** – the leaf is allowed to dry and is broken to allow fermentation, either by
3 **Rolling** or by
4 **Crushing** and **tearing.** The tea is now ready for
5 **Fermentation:** it is left for a time to ferment, then
6 **Firing** – changes the colour to black, by drying the leaves with hot air.
7 **Grading** – sorts the leaves into large and small.
8 **Transporting** – the tea is packed in boxes and sent all over the world.
9 **Tasting** – when it arrives it is tasted, to check its flavour and quality.
10 **Selling** – the different types of tea are sold in a tea market, and then mixed together to make the tea we drink.

Essential steps in the growth and manufacture of tea

ORTHODOX ROLLING or . . .

PLUCKING—Only two leaves and a bud are gathered. The tea is then taken directly to the processing factory for . . .

WITHERING, this reduces the moisture in the leaf which is then ruptured to induce fermentation by one of two methods either . . .

CRUSH, TEAR and CURL. The latter process produces a smaller leaf. The tea is now ready for the . . .

FERMENTATION room where it is stored in a balanced atmospheric condition until reaching optimum colour and quality . . .

FIRING—At the crucial moment fermentation is halted by hot air drying the tea, resulting in the familiar black tea colour . . .

After firing, the tea passes through vibrating sieves GRADING the now black tea to various leaf sizes. Packed into tea chests . . .

and palletized to facilitate quick loading by fork lift trucks, the tea is SHIPPED to Britain and other Countries . . .

On arrival it is stored in warehouses. Expert TEA TASTERS sample for quality . . .

all the teas offered for AUCTION.

On reaching the tea packing factory, as many as thirty different teas are blended to make up such famous brands as P.G. Tips. This ensures that the housewife's favourite blends are always consistent in quality.

17 Narrative/telling a story

A Text

24 INCHES FROM DEATH

By WILLIAM DANIELS

SCHOOLBOY Jonathon Vowles was all smiles last night after cheating death by just twenty-four inches.

Jonathon's miracle escape came when he made his first parachute jump.

Excitement turned to horror after he leapt from a plane at 2,500 feet.

FIRST his main parachute failed to open.

THEN his emergency 'chute wrapped round his body as he corkscrewed towards the ground.

In a crazy free fall that lasted forty-five seconds the 16-year-old boy hurtled towards the metal roof of an aircraft hanger.

Dangling

He appeared doomed. But then came the miracle.

Instead of slamming on to the roof. Jonathon smashed through a tiny skylight. His parachute cords caught on the broken window frame . . . and he was jerked to a sudden halt with his feet dangling two feet from the ground.

His only injury was strained ligaments caused by the parachute harness twisting round his right leg as his plunge was stopped.

Fairhaired Jonathon said at his home in Corve Street, Ludlow, Shropshire:

' I can't believe I was so lucky. I couldn't have picked a better place to land if I'd aimed for it.

' It was my first and last parachute jump — I don't think I'll ever try it again.

'I can still see the white faces of my school pals looking down at me as I lay on a stretcher.

'Six of us made the jump, and I was the last to go. I don't remember much after that. But I know my chute didn't open, and I dropped right past the boy who had gone before me.

'I was too busy going through the emergency procedure to think about what was going to happen to me. But the next thing I knew I had gone through the window in the hanger roof and I was hanging just above the ground.

'I was very embarrassed because I couldn't stop my legs shaking while people were cutting me free.

The youngsters, all from Ludlow comprehensive school, had two days' training before they made their jump from a Cessna plane over Shobden airfield near Leominster.

Jonathon's mother, Mrs. Olivia Vowles, said: 'It's a miracle he's alive. The whole thing was incredible, and I'm glad I wasn't there to see it.

'Just going to the hospital to see him put years on me.'

B Vocabulary

cheating death	= escaping from death
corkscrewed	= turned round and round, in a spiral
hurtled	= fell very quickly
hangar	= garage for aeroplanes
doomed	= going to die
skylight	= small window in the roof
dangling	= hanging
plunge	= fall

C Comprehension

1 What was Jonathon twenty-four inches away from?
2 Why was it called a miracle escape?
3 Why didn't he come down slowly like his friends?
4 What did he injure? Was it serious or not?
5 Is he going to make another parachute jump?

D Analysis

1 Why did Jonathon and his friends go parachuting?
  Who was organising it?
2 How did everybody feel as they watched Jonathon fall?
3 What would have happened if he hadn't hit the skylight?

E Inference

1 Why do you think both his parachutes failed? Could there be a special reason, or was it just bad luck?
2 Jonathon says that he was going through the emergency procedure when he fell — what could this be?

F Discussion

1 Parachuting is obviously very dangerous — so why do you think many people want to do it?
2 This story was on the front page of a national newspaper (*The Daily Mirror*). Why did the newspaper think it was an important story? Would it have been such an important story if Jonathon had been killed? What makes some stories more important than others — from the newspaper's point of view?

G Language Practice

1 Describing feelings

Here are some of the words used in the text to describe how the people felt or reacted to the situation:

Positive	Negative
all smiles	horror
excitement	white faces
lucky	embarrassed
it's incredible	it put years on me (ie it made me feel old)

These words describe the emotions that people felt in the story. When telling a story that involves people, it's important to include a description of how they felt.

Here are some more words that Jonathon could have used to describe his feelings. Use them to complete the text underneath.*

Positive	Negative
happy	frightened
relieved	terrified
excited	apprehensive
grateful	worried
glad	nervous

'I was a little . . . before we went up in the aeroplane, because I knew it was dangerous. The others were a little . . . too, but also very . . . . I wasn't . . . when I jumped, and for the first few seconds I felt . . . I'd had the courage to try. When I realised the parachute hadn't opened, I was . . ., and thought about what it would be like to hit the ground. I was . . . that I would feel my bones breaking. I don't remember much more until I woke up in hospital. I'm very . . . to the doctors and nurses there — they were nice. I'm very . . . it's all over, and only a little . . . that I didn't have time to enjoy the jump properly.

2 Intensifying

Some words seem stronger than others, although their meaning is really the same, or nearly the same. When you are telling a story, these words help to make it more interesting:

Neutral	Strong
to jump	leap
to fall, go towards	hurtle
to break	smash
to pull	jerk
fall	plunge
fear	horror
unbelievable	incredible

Use some of these words to make this text more interesting, by exaggerating a little with strong words:*

> Jack Crowhurst was driving down one of Scotland's highest mountains, when he noticed that his brakes weren't working. A look of fear came to his face. He pulled on the handbrake hard, but nothing happened. It was unbelievable, but true – he couldn't slow the car down. He made a quick decision. He pulled the door open, and jumped out, rolling into the road. As he lay there he saw the car go downhill very quickly, and then fall over the edge of the road. He couldn't see anything, but he heard it break into a thousand pieces at the bottom of the mountain.

H Writing Practice

1 Setting the scene

An important part of telling a story is the beginning – it must make people interested. There are two ways to set the scene, to start the story off. One is to describe the scene itself: – the place/time/weather/people involved. The other is to give the reader a 'taste' of what the story is going to be about. This is done in the text at the beginning of the unit:

> Schoolboy Jonathon Vowles was all smiles last night after cheating death by just twenty-four inches.

Now practise setting the scene by changing the beginning of that text, and writing an introduction that describes the scene before Jonathon fell.

To practise the second method, re-write the beginning of this text to give a 'taste' of what is going to happen.

> It was a lovely clear summer's day, and thousands of tourists were enjoying breakfast in the airport's restaurants. Many watched the planes coming and going, and saw the Jumbo for Australia speed down the runway and take off. As they turned to watch it climb, there was a scream of horror. Another plane had appeared out of nowhere, and was flying across the path of the Jumbo. There was a huge flash of fire, and the windows of the restaurant shook with the explosion as the two planes crashed in mid-air.
>
> There were no survivors.

2 Creating suspense

Suspense is the feeling of not knowing what the end of a story is going to be – it creates excitement and interest. You can do it by leaving the important information to the end – not like the text about Jonathon, which tells you at the beginning that he has escaped. So it's not always a good idea to give a 'taste' of what is going to happen – it can spoil the suspense.

To practise this, write a short summary of the parachute story, giving the basic facts. But don't explain that he survived, or how he did it, until the last two or three sentences.

3 Personal accounts

The short texts above are mainly impersonal. It is usually more interesting if a story is told by someone who was there, or who is describing what they have seen or done. Personal accounts don't just use 'I' instead of 'he' – they are more informal, and describe feelings more strongly. For example, look at this sentence from the text on Jack Crowhurst:

A look of fear came to his face.

Jack can't write this about himself, so he would write:

I was terrified *or*

I felt very frightened

Now practise this by re-writing this story about Geoff trying to sell his house. You are Geoff – explain what happened:

Lucky for some .. it's No. 12A

By CLIVE CRICKMER

GEOFF and Anne Pearce had high hopes of selling their smart modern house quickly . . . until their number came up.

The house at Welburn Close, Ovingham, Northumberland, seemed a bargain at £12,500 and there were plenty of would-be buyers.

But each inquiry dried up when 30-year-old Geoff revealed that the number of the house, which had been advertised by name, was 13.

Then the number was changed to 12A — and Geoff got a firm bid within days.

I Writing Tasks

1 Write the story of some event that you have experienced – a disaster, or a good experience, or something humorous. (150-200 words)

2 Imagine you have interviewed someone famous. Now write the story of their life. (100-150 words)

3 Read this newspaper report, and then re-write it as a personal account, from Paul's point of view. Include the conversations he had with people. (100-150 words)

Smash hit hero

Paul Scofield was a smash hit in Guildford yesterday, saving two young girls in a runaway car – but wrecking his own car in the process.

Paul, a salesman from London, was driving past a Rover parked outside a supermarket, when he saw it start to roll slowly down the hill. Inside the car were two young girls on the passenger seat – but no driver. Paul stopped quickly, jumped in front of the Rover and tried to stop it, pushing against the front of the car. Another passer-by got into the car and put on the handbrake, saving the girls from certain injury.

It was at this point that Paul noticed his own car, rolling slowly down the hill – and going too fast for him to stop it. It crashed into a bus at the bottom of the hill, and was so badly damaged that it had to be towed away to a garage.

As if this was not bad enough, Paul now finds he has no-one to blame. He was so busy chasing his car that he didn't get the name of the driver of the Rover, who just came out of the supermarket and drove away without realising what had happened.

4 This picture shows a copy of the old ships that brought Vikings from Norway to Britain. It is being sailed from Norway to Britain again to mark 1000 years of history. Imagine you were on the boat. Describe what happened on the journey, and also when the people welcomed you on the Isle of Man – the end of the journey. (150-200 words)

18 Expressing opinions

A Text

> **THE BEACH BOYS: " L.A. (Light Album" (Columbia JZ35752, U.S. import).**
>
> The good releases couldn't go on for ever, so here's a really duff one to balance the picture. The Beach Boys are one of the greatest bands in the history of rock, but with their last few albums they have clearly run out of inspiration. This one is the worst yet. Their single *Here Comes The Night*, was a faster, disco-ish re-make of the song from the '67 classic *Wild Honey*, and was pretty dreadful. Heard on the album, it comes over as one of the better tracks. Most of the first side is slow, gentle, slushy and soporific.
>
> It's pleasant, certainly, if you want to fall asleep or need insipid but well-performed background music. But it's not what the wonderful Beach Boys used to be about.

B Vocabulary

album — LP record
release — record
duff — bad, low quality (slang)
run out of — no longer have any
inspiration — ideas
disco-ish — discotheque – style music
re-make — a new version
comes over — gives the impression, seems to be
slushy — sentimental (in a negative way)
soporific — it sends you to sleep
insipid — weak, with no character

C Comprehension

1 What does the writer think of the Beach Boys' new record?
2 What sort of record is it – single or LP?
3 What did the writer think of the Beach Boys before this record?
4 What is the difference between *Here comes the Night* and the other songs on the LP
5 What good things does the writer say about the music?

D Analysis

1 What is the purpose of this text? Where do you think it comes from? What is the name for it?
2 What does the writer think is the problem of the Beach Boys? Why has he changed his opinion?
3 How can you find out the writer's opinions about the group and the music? Underline the parts of the text that express an opinion.

E Inference

1 What is *Wild Honey*, or what might it be?
2 The writer says 'It's not what the wonderful Beach Boys used to be about'. What do you think the writer feels they *used* to be about?

F Discussion

1 What do you think is the purpose of criticism like this? Is it to help people choose records? Is it to make the critic famous?
2 Is it possible to describe music in words like this? Do you take any notice of criticisms or reviews before you buy records?
3 Some people would say it is a waste of time to write a review of a pop record, as pop music is not serious, and only lasts a few weeks. What do you think of this viewpoint?

G Language Practice

1 Expressing an opinion

If you think something is good, you can express your opinion simply:

It's good

To make it clear that this is *your* opinion, and to make your conversation and writing more interesting, there are several phrases you can use to introduce your opinion:

I think that. . .
In my opinion,. . .
I would say that. . .
As far as I'm concerned. . .
The point is that. . .

Now use these phrases to give your opinion on these topics:

a flying men to the moon   d rock music
b drinking alcohol   e EEC membership
c vegetarianism

2 Tentative opinions

If you are not sure what your opinion is, or it's not very definite, you can use these words and phrases to show that:

I'm not sure that. . .
perhaps it's a question of. . .
maybe the reason is. . .
some people would say that. . .

Now practise using these, and give a tentative (unsure) opinion on these topics:

a strikes
b killing animals for fur-coats
c nuclear power
d the need for homework at school

H Writing Practice

1 Analysing opinions

As well as expressing your own opinion, you must be able to work out what opinions other people are expressing. Look at these two texts and one cartoon, and write a description of the opinion that the writer is expressing – or what you think he/she is expressing. In each one, explain what it is that makes you think this is the opinion the writer had.

a What does the writer think about the film?

FILM GUIDE

COLCHESTER
Odeon. — Screen One:
The Terror of Dr Chaney (X) Sunday for seven days. Small wonder this nasty little horror had to wait almost five years for a general release. It will do nothing for established artists like Richard Basehart as the mad medico who kidnaps unsuspecting victims to try to transplant their eyes to restore the sight of his daughter — blinded in a car crash for which he was responsible — or Gloria Grahame, his unlucky nurse. The picture stumbles around as sightlessly as its grotesque characters.

b What does the writer think about the record? How is this opinion different from the one is the text at the beginning of the unit?

The sound of the album is beautiful, because the band has always written with a love for beautiful changes, because the harmonies are as well-sung as ever, and because the production, by Jim Guercio and Bruce Johnston strives unashamedly to please the ear. The song which has received most attention is "Here Comes The Night," a ten-minute disco version (with added arrangements by Bob Esty) of the tune from "Wild Honey."

The rest of "L.A." is comprised of short, melancholy, exquisite ballads. "Angel Come Home" is a great pop record on an old theme. "Good Timin'" and "Full Sail" are songs with positive messages that make you feel sad; its clear how imperfect we are, how pathologically misunderstanding and mis-understood, how seeing the light and employing it are not the same thing. That they communicate irony without bitterness, sadness without hopelessness, is the mark of their art.

DAVITT SIGERSON.

c What is the cartoonist's opinion about libraries/ the people who work there/reading books? What does he want you to think?

2 Responding to opinions

When you read or hear other people's opinions, you usually want to respond by giving your own opinion about the same subject. You can do this by agreeing or disagreeing (see Unit 19) or by simply stating what you think, and let other people analyse whether you are agreeing or disagreeing. For example:

Opinion: I think all murderers should be hung
Your opinion: I think the real problem is finding out why people commit murders in the first place

Here are some useful phrases:

Surely the main point is. . .
The *real* problem seems to be. . .
I tend to think. . .
What we *should* be worrying about is. . .

Practise responding in this way to the following opinions you have read or heard. Write them down as if they were part of a letter to a newspaper or TV programme:

a Government documents should be available for everyone to see.

b All children should stay at school until they are eighteen.

c No-one should be allowed to have more than one house or one car – the world is too short of resources.

Don't write more than about 50-80 words in giving your opinion.

I Writing Tasks

1 Give your personal opinion about a film or concert you have seen, and advise someone else to see it (or not, if it is no good!). (150 words)

2 Choose your favourite books or records and write a serious (formal) review of them, explaining why they are good. (150 words)

3 You have just been to a football match or similar exciting sporting event. Write a letter to a friend who likes the same sport, giving your opinion of it. (100-150 words)

4 The town you live in has a lot of problems – not enough car parks, little entertainment etc. Write a letter to the local authorities giving your opinion on how it could be improved. (150-200 words)

5 This letter and cartoon appeared in the newspaper. It gives a humorous opinion about the use of ties. Write a letter to the newspaper replying to this letter, giving your opinion on this subject. (100-150 words)

Why men should try to loosen the ties of oppressive tradition

Sir, — Now that women are to be allowed to wear dress that is both comfortable and practical may we expect the Equal Opportunities Commission to turn its attention to us men, oppressed by society's slavish obedience to tradition.

It could make a start with the tie, a garment which serves no conceivable purpose whatsoever, is troublesome to tie just right without seemingly glaring wrinkles in the knot, and necessitates a buttoned-up collar, which is uncomfortable and restrictive at the best of times, but almost unbearable in hot summer weather. — Yours faithfully,

Clive G. Davis,
Badock Hall,
Stoke Park Road,
Bristol.

---

19 Agreeing/disagreeing

A Text

THE OBSERVER, SUNDAY 18 FEBRUARY 1979   **Feiffer**

B Vocabulary

gibble	=	an invented word, replacing the name of things to buy, etc
rush out	=	hurry out
heed	=	pay attention to
raise children	=	bring up children
cults	=	group of people who believe the same thing – usually a religious group
threat	=	possible problem or danger

C Comprehension

1 What do the television, teacher, priest, etc have in common? What are they doing?

2 What are the two children/two adults doing in each picture?

3 What are they learning in each situation? What does the writer/cartoonist think they are learning?

4 What happens to the two children in the eight pictures? What is this supposed to show?

5 At one point the boy and girl are shown separately – why is this?

D Analysis

1 Look again at each picture, and summarise what is happening to the children. Try to find the word or words that could replace 'gibble'.
2 Which influence does the writer think is most strong in everybody's life?

E Inference

1 The text of the last picture has an implied, or hidden meaning – what is it? What is the writer saying?
2 The title of this TV programme can be called 'ironic' – explain why.

F Discussion

1 Do you think the TV and teachers and the church and magazines try to influence how we think? Is the writer's idea a good one, or exaggerated?
2 Do you think a lot of people watch TV all the time, like the people in the cartoon? Do you?

G Language Practice

1 Agreeing

Agreeing is showing a positive response to someone's opinion – it might just mean nodding your head. But when you're writing, you want to show that you agree with something that was said or written before. So you need to re-state the opinion as well:

> *I agree that* football is a waste of time.
> The idea that TV influences us is *of course quite right*.
> *I share the opinion of* Mr Smith, who said all pop music is rubbish.
> *I'd like to add my support* to the people who want to change the drinking laws.

Now use these sentences to agree with and re-state these opinions from a radio discussion programme:*

a No family should have more than two children.
b All education should be free.
c There should be no borders between countries.
d English should be taught in all schools.

2 Disagreeing

When you are speaking, disagreeing is easy. You say 'That's not right' or 'I don't agree with that'. But when you are writing, you need to re-state the opinion, so the person you are writing to can understand. Here are some examples:

> *It's ridiculous to say* that English should be taught everywhere.
> *I disagree with* people who believe that. . .
> *I can't accept the idea that*. . .
> *I think you're wrong* to believe that. . .

Now practise using these sentences, by disagreeing with these opinions. You have received a letter from your boss, telling you he wants to sack you for these reasons:*

a You are always late for work.
b You never do the job properly.
c You persuade the other workers to ask for more money.
d You don't have any respect for your employers.

H Writing Practice

1 For and Against

When you are discussing or writing about a subject, you can often divide the opinions and arguments into two groups – for and against, the good points and the bad points of the topic.

For example, here are the arguments/opinions we could put under *Against* if we write about the subject of Television:

Against:

a TV influences how we think.
b TV advertisements tell us what to buy.
c Watching TV means sitting down – it's unhealthy.
d Watching TV stops people thinking for themselves or making their own entertainment.

2 Now try and make a similar list of arguments about the *good* points of television –

For : a, b, c etc
Make a table of *For* and *Against* points for two of these topics:
   frozen food
   motorways
   an armed police force
Make a table like this:

For	Against

3 From this *For* and *Against* table, about the killing of whales, write full sentences about the subject. Show where you agree or disagree:

Against	For
a killing whales is cruel	a Eskimos have always killed whales
b whales are dying out– there are not many left	b Eskimos live off whale meat
c killing whales disturbs the balance of life in the sea	c Eskimos need whale fat to heat their homes
d whale killing should be banned	d whale killing should not be banned for Eskimos

I Writing Tasks

1 Write a composition about the advantages and disadvantages of owning a motorbike instead of a car. (120-180 words)

2 'It's better to have a job with a lot of free time, but not much money, rather than to have a job with a lot of money, but not much free time'. Write a composition to agree or disagree with this opinion. Explain the advantages of your viewpoint. (150-200 words)

3 Look at this story from a San Francisco newspaper:

Sue Sued by Courting Tom

Tom Dixon was very angry when his girlfriend didn't arrive at the restaurant. They had arranged to meet at seven to have dinner, and then go to the theatre. But Susan Kovacs didn't turn up – she had gone out with someone else.

So Tom decided to go to court, and he sued Susan for 50 dollars – the cost of his petrol, the theatre tickets, and his time waiting for her. He says she broke a contract by not arriving.

Now imagine the conversation between Tom and Susan as they explain this to the judge. Write down how they agree and disagree, and write what you think the judge would agree with. (150-200 words)

4 Imagine you have just interviewed a famous sportsman. He has told you about the good and bad points of being famous – eg a lot of money for wearing the names of cigarette companies on his jacket. Write the interview as a composition, where you agree or disagree with what Jonny Connell, tennis star, told you. (150--200 words)

5 This letter appeared in the newspaper. You disagree with it very strongly – write a reply, addressed to the Editor of the newspaper. It should be a formal letter. (120-180 words)

Sir, – I think it is disgusting that this town has increased the cost of using the car parks. It is very difficult to park anywhere, because of the stupid No Parking signs. We pay a lot of money in taxes to pay for roads - then the Government closes the roads so silly pedestrians can go shopping.

We should be allowed to park anywhere, free, and drive anywhere in the city. Cars need more freedom!

HAROLD BAKER
London, SW14.

20 Building an argument
A Text

SINGLE AND SOLVENT

One of the best reasons for being single is the freedom it gives you to spend your own money in your own way. Wine, women and song – in that order – seem to figure large in male expenditure while clothes, cosmetics and males seem to account for a great deal of female salaries.

SINGLE AND FANCY-FREE

The other good reason for being single is the amount of free time you have to enjoy in any way you prefer. Not for singles the chores of family shopping and doing odd jobs about the house. Not for them the worries about baby-sitters to get one night out a week.

Singles are free to spend their time just as the mood takes them. They can roller skate; go to the pictures; explore old ruins or just sit with their feet up and enjoy the innocent sin of being completely indolent. They can get up when they like and go to bed when they like. Eat where, what and when they fancy. And meet whoever they like as often as they like.

Single people are very lucky financially. And if you don't believe it – ask a married friend.

The freedom is great. And if you don't believe it – ask a married friend.

B Vocabulary

solvent	=	without money problems
to figure large	=	to be important
expenditure	=	spending
fancy-free	=	with no worries
chores	=	boring household jobs
roller skate	=	skate on two pieces of wood, with wheels
pictures	=	slang for cinema
indolent	=	lazy

C Comprehension

1 Who is the writer comparing single people with? Which group does he think has a better life?
2 What are the main reasons for staying single?
3 What do single people do that married people don't, or can't do?
4 What does the picture suggest about the single life? Is it realistic?
5 What does the writer suggest you should do if you don't believe him? Why?

D Analysis

1 Do you think the writer is single or married? How can you tell?
2 What group of people is this text written for? What do you think the purpose is? To persuade people to stay single?

E Inference

This text is in fact part of an advertisement for a computer dating service. The service will take details about you, and find friends of the opposite sex for you – if you pay the charges. Why do you think they start the advertisement saying how wonderful it is to be single? Wouldn't it be better to suggest they need a husband/wife? What do you think?

F Discussion

1 The text suggests there is a difference in the way single men and women spend their money. Do you agree? Or is this an exaggerated opinion?
2 Many people pay a lot of money to this computer service, in order to find a boyfriend/girlfriend who has the same interests etc. Why do they do this, instead of meeting people normally? What do you think of it?

G Language Practice

1 Connectors

Some words are very useful to connect ideas together:

Although cassettes are improving, they don't give very good quality sound.
Records give good quality sound, *therefore* are better for classical music.
Since records give better sound, they are better for classical music.
Cassettes, *however*, do have the advantage of being small.

Each of these words – *although, therefore, since, however* – is used in a different way. Look at the examples again and then fill the gaps in these sentences with the same words:*

Heavy lorries cause a lot of damage to our roads, and . . . are very unpopular. Many people suggest that the goods could go by train, . . . trains do not damage roads. Not every town has a station, . . ., so . . . this sounds like a good idea, it doesn't actually work.

2 These sentences are in the right order, but need to be connected, using the words *although/therefore/because/which/however/but**

a many cinemas were in danger of closing
b most people preferred to stay at home
c there has been an improvement recently
d this improvement is very welcome
e this improvement has helped many cinemas
f there used to be good films on TV
g people stayed at home
h the situation now is very different
i the TV bosses will not admit it

Try to make only three sentences out of this list, by using the connectors.

H Writing Practice

1 Planning

When you are writing a composition, you must have a plan. This is especially important if your composition is expressing your opinion, putting forward an argument or comparing the *For* and *Against* points of a topic. A good plan makes it easier to write – and easier to read. Look at the text again, and pick out the reasons for staying single.

Now look at this plan for a composition 'Why you should stay single':

Introduction: Many people believe that staying single is better than getting married.
Why is it so popular?
Main point 1: Financial freedom – you can spend your money in any way.
What do single people do with their money?
Compare with expensive married life – babies, houses etc.
Main point 2: Freedom of time – you can do what you want at any time.
You can choose what you want to do, when, where, and with whom you want to do it.
Conclusion: If you want to travel, have a good time, spend money on yourself, it's best to stay single.

2 For and Against

From this plan you can write a good composition. Practise making plans, first, by writing a plan like this one for the topic:
'Why you should get married'
Some ideas to use – loneliness/share things/fun with children/happy old age.

Another sort of plan would be a *For* and *Against* plan, that brings the two topics together and discusses the advantages and disadvantages, and then comes to a conclusion in the same way.
Here is an example:
Title: 'Is marriage worthwhile?'
Introduction: Many people deciding to stay single, for different reasons (give examples).
For: Advantages of being single, and problems of being married.
Against: Problems of being single – good things about marriage.
Conclusion: Personal feeling – what I would prefer to do.

Now practise making a plan like this for the topic:
'Is it worth going to University – or should I get a job after leaving school?'

3 Paragraphing

Using paragraphs instead of one long piece of text makes a composition easier to read. Look at the text at the beginning of the unit – it has five paragraphs, which split up the different ideas. Each paragraph has a different idea, or a different way of looking at an idea. When you come to the end of a paragraph, there is a natural pause – so it's easier to read.

Practise separating text into paragraphs by rewriting this news story. It should be in five short paragraphs. Re-write it and start each paragraph on a new line.

Women teachers won a battle yesterday – the battle of the trousers. They were banned from school for one day last week because they refused to wear skirts or dresses. The headmaster, James Dinsley, had said that no trousers were allowed, because it gave a bad example to girls at the school. Both the male and female teachers thought that this was ridiculous, and so all the women in the school protested. After a long meeting between the teachers, the headmaster and officials from the education authority, the headmaster had to change his mind. 'It's a victory for commonsense' said one of the teachers. 'We're glad it's all over and we can get some work done.'

I Writing Tasks

1 Make a plan as in Section H2 above and write a composition on the advantages and problems of nuclear power stations. (200-250 words)

2 Over-population and hunger are big problems. Write a plan (as in Section H1) and a composition about what you think could be done about the problem. (150-200 words)

3 'Computers will help us create a much better world in the future'. Write a composition agreeing *or* disagreeing with this idea. Give your reasons. (150-200 words)

4 'Should divorce be made easier or more difficult?' Write a composition arguing the view you believe in. (120-180 words)

Key to exercises

Unit 1

1 a Glad you're enjoying yourself.
  b Hope you can drop in.
  c Been working hard this week.
  d Got any money?
  e Like a cigarette?

2 a I'm saving my money.
  b She's bought a new car.
  c They couldn't help me.
  d We're going to America.
  e They've painted their house.

Unit 2

1 a I enjoy listening to records, but I prefer to go to a concert.
  b I enjoy watching TV but I prefer to go out.
  c I enjoy going to a football match, but I prefer to play football.
  d I enjoy eating meat, but I prefer to live on vegetarian food.
  e I enjoy having a bath but I prefer to take a shower.

2 a I have been learning Spanish for two years.
  b John has been living in London for twenty years.
  c We have been attending this school for ten days.
  d I have been staying in Bournemouth for a week.
  e Sally has been playing guitar for a year.

Unit 3

1 a extremely /very
  b not cheap/quite expensive
  c very popular/popular
  d very good/quite good
  e not stupid/quite clever
  f rather

Unit 4

1 a There are two bathrooms, both upstairs.
  b There is a garden with a very large lawn.
  c There is a good shopping centre in the town.
    There are two cinemas in the town.
  d There is a cloakroom to the right of the lobby.
  e There are a lot of fitted cupboards in the kitchen.

Unit 5

1 a The Games were stopped by the Romans in 393.
  b Many different games were played by the sportsmen.
  c The Games were seen by fifty thousand people in 1896.
  d The Games were cancelled by the organisers in 1916.

2 a People used to watch the Games beneath Mount Olympus.
  b The Greeks used to stop their wars to go to the Games.
  c Women used not to be allowed to join in the Games.
  d The Olympics used to be held every five years.

Unit 6

1 (suggested answers—there can be many of this form)
  a The Coral is cheaper than the Bella.
  b The Coral is not as fast as the Bella.
  c The Bella has power-assisted steering, whereas the Coral only has normal steering.
  d Although the Bella is more expensive, it is cheaper to buy its spare parts.

2 (suggested answers—there can be many of this form)
  a Not only has the Coral got more doors, it has a free carpet as well.
  b On the one hand the Coral is very cheap, but on the other hand it's very noisy.

Unit 7

(suggested answers)
1 a Would you like to come on a picnic?
  b How about going to the sea for the weekend?
  c I'm going to the theatre on Friday — would you like to come?
  d How would you like to go for a meal, and then to a discotheque?

2 a I'd love to come, but I've arranged something.
  b Thanks all the same, but I'm visiting some friends.
  c That's very kind, but I've got to work.
  d I'd love to come, but I'm meeting some friends.

Unit 8

1 (suggested answers)
  a I'd rather have a Rolls.
  b I prefer brown bread.
  c I'd prefer to be a politician.
  d I'd rather have more money and less time.

2 a Cowboy films are interesting, whereas love stories are very boring.
  b Beethoven's music is of good quality, whereas pop music is all rubbish.
  c Travelling by car is fast and expensive, whereas walking is cheap and slow.
  d Although Jim had no money, he went to Bali on holiday.
  e Although Alan was very lazy at school, he passed his exams.

Unit 9

1 a You have to insert the film into the camera.
  b You have to wind the film on to number 1.
  c You have to set the aperture.
  d You have to open the lens cover.
  e You have a look at the subject through the view-finder.

2 a The film should be inserted into the camera.
  b The film should be wound on to number 1.
  c The aperture should be set.
  d The lens cover should be opened.
  e The subject should be looked at through the view-finder.

Unit 10

(suggested answers)
1 — we're going to reduce taxes.
  — we're going to improve the hospital service.
  — we're going to build more houses.
  — we're hoping to keep prices as low as possible.
  — we're hoping to stop the building of nuclear power stations.
  — we're planning to increase pensions.
  — we're planning to stop the use of animals in experiments.
  — we're hoping to make the cities safe at night.
  — we're hoping to plan for a safe future.

2 (personal opinions)

Unit 11

1   This post offers a considerable salary and gives a good opportunity to someone who wishes to obtain good experience. We require people who are enthusiastic and hard-working. Selling experience is preferred.

2 a Having learned Spanish, I want to visit South America.
  b Having failed his exams, he went back to school.
  c Having taken the Civil Service tests, she had an interview.
  d Teaching in a school, he knows a lot about children.

Unit 12

1 a He shouldn't have been following the lorry closely.
  b He shouldn't have been looking out of the side-window.
  c He shouldn't have been driving without a seat-belt.
  d The brakes shouldn't have been making a strange noise.

2 a The windscreen wipers should have been working properly.
  b He should have been concentrating on the road.
  c The lorry should have been using good tyres.
  d He should have been driving under 40 mph.

Unit 13

1 a The woman, whose husband was killed in a car crash, sold her sports car today.
  b The town, whose football team won the FA Cup, has given a special dinner for the footballers.
  c Sir Lawrence Olivier, whose acting is known all over the world, received an Oscar award.
  d Roberto Leone, whose paintings of the Queen made him famous, died today.
  e The pop group Cannon, whose new record is at the top of the charts, have refused to appear on television.

2 a The workers were warned today about the strike.
  b New taxes have been introduced by the Government.
  c Ten people were killed yesterday in a car crash.
  d A woman has lost her dog in the forest.
  e The theatre is to close if no money is found.

Unit 14

(suggested answers)
1 a If you want to go to university, you'd better pass your examinations.
  b If he wants to work in the USA, he should get a work permit first.
  c If you want to be successful, you ought to get up early.
  d If they want to make a lot of money, they should start their own business.

2 a You should go on a diet.
  b Why don't you save a little each month?
  c You could wear more clothes.
  d You should buy a new one.

Unit 15

(suggested answers)

1 a Why don't we have a dinner party?
  b Let's go camping in Wales.
  c Why don't you try Donaldson's soups?
  d I suggest we meet to discuss business.
  e You should buy Suno TV sets.

2 a You must go camping – it's wonderful.
  b You really ought to go on a diet.
  c Don't you think you should buy this LP? It's amazing.
  d You'll really enjoy learning to play the piano.
  e Perhaps you ought to buy a cassette recorder.

Unit 16

1 a The wheat must be planted in May.
  b The wheat is harvested in September.
  c It is transported to the mill.
  d It must be ground into flour.
  e The flour is taken to the bakery.
  f The flour and other things are baked into bread.

2 a After being turned on, the gas is lit.
  b Before being placed on the cooker, the pan is filled with water.
  c As soon as the water has boiled, the pan is taken off.
  d As soon as the tealeaves are put into the pot, hot water is poured over the tea.
  e After being left for two minutes, the tea is served.

Unit 17

1 I was a little apprehensive before we went up in the aeroplane because I knew it was dangerous. The others were a little nervous too, but also very excited. I wasn't frightened when I jumped, and for the first few seconds I felt glad I'd had the courage to try. When I realised the parachute hadn't opened, I was terrified, and thought about what it would be like to hit the ground. I was worried that I would feel my bones breaking. I don't remember much more until I woke up in hospital. I'm very grateful to the doctors and nurses there – they were very nice. I'm very happy it's all over, and only a little disappointed that I didn't have time to enjoy the jump properly.

2 Jack Crowhurst was driving down one of Scotland's highest mountains when he noticed that his brakes weren't working. A look of horror came to his face. He jerked on the handbrake hard but nothing happened. It was incredible – but true, he couldn't slow the car down. He made a quick decision. He jerked the door open and leaped out, rolling into the road. As he lay there he saw the car hurtle downhill and then plunge over the edge of the road. He couldn't see anything but he heard it smash into a thousand pieces at the bottom of the mountain.

Unit 19

(suggested answers)

1 a I agree that no family should have more than two children.
  b I'd like to add my support to those who think all education should be free.
  c I share the opinion that there should be no borders between countries.
  d It is of course quite right that English should be taught in all schools.

2 a I can't accept that I'm always late for work.
  b It's ridiculous to say I never do the job properly.
  c I disagree that I persuade other workers to ask for more money.
  d I think you're wrong to believe I don't have any respect for my employers.

Unit 20

1 Heavy lorries cause a lot of damage to our roads and therefore are very unpopular. Many people suggest that the goods could go by train, since trains do not damage roads. Not every town has a station, however, so although this sounds like a good idea, it doesn't actually work.

2 a Although many cinemas were in danger of closing because most people preferred to stay at home, there has been an improvement recently.
  b This improvement, which has helped many cinemas, is very welcome.
  c Because there used to be good films on TV, people stayed at home, but the situation now, however, is very different, although the TV bosses will not admit it.